DIGITAL IMMORTALITY

Bookarion

DIGITAL IMMORTALITY

Transferring Human Personality to Artificial Intelligence and Humanoid Robots

Taner TAŞKIRAN

ISBN: 978-625-96380-1-0
e-ISBN: 978-625-96380-2-7

June 2026

Editor
Tuğba ATAMTÜRK

Publishing Coordinator
Dr. Dilek KURBAN

Academic Consultant
Assoc. Prof. Dr. Elvan ATAMTÜRK

Cover, Interior Design & E-Book
Bookarion Visual Arts

Bookarion

Seyrantepe Mah. Gökdeniz Sok. No:15/3
34413 – Kâğıthane – İstanbul – Türkiye
www.bookarion.com info@bookarion.com

bookarion bookarion bookarion bookarion bookarion
bookarion bookarion bookarion bookarion bookarion

Bookarion *and* **Bookarion Scholar** *are publishing imprints of Smart and Start Intelligent Financial Solutions Consulting and Publishing Inc...*

DIGITAL IMMORTALITY

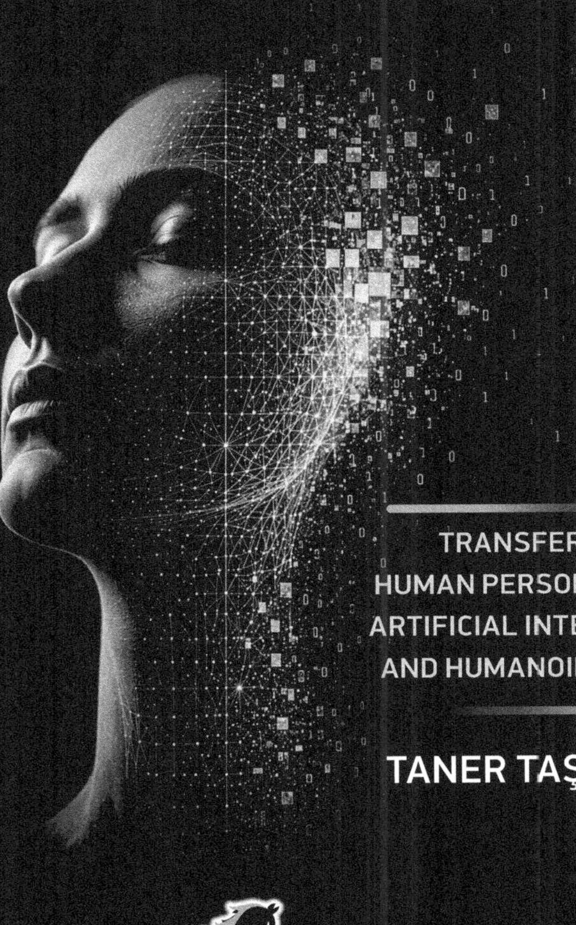

TRANSFERRING HUMAN PERSONALITY TO ARTIFICIAL INTELLIGENCE AND HUMANOID ROBOTS

TANER TAŞKIRAN

Bookarion

PREFACE

Since the dawn of time, humanity has pursued the dream of immortality. This quest, deeply rooted in mythology, religion, and literature, has now evolved into a new dimension with the advent of modern technology. Artificial intelligence and humanoid robots are no longer mere tools to simplify our lives; they hold the potential to answer one of humanity's greatest questions: "Is death truly the end?"

This book explores the concept of copying human personality, consciousness, and emotions into artificial intelligence and humanoid robots, enabling them to live on in a new form. Digital immortality has transcended the realm of science fiction and become a groundbreaking reality at the intersection of science and technology. This transformative journey engages disciplines such as biology, psychology, artificial intelligence, robotics, and ethics, offering both extraordinary opportunities and profound challenges.

While writing this book, I addressed fundamental questions: Can human personality be digitally reproduced? Does transferring our thoughts and memories into artificial intelligence or humanoid robots ensure the continuity of the individual? What are the ethical, legal, and societal implications of digital immortality?

To answer these questions, I combined theoretical insights supported by scientific research with forward-looking scenarios and thought-provoking discussions. I aimed to illuminate the philosophical and human dimensions of digital immortality while inspiring readers to consider its implications.

This book is not only for scientists and technology enthusiasts but also for those intrigued by the ethical, philosophical, and societal questions that will shape our future. The subject at hand is not just a technological matter; it is a revolution that redefines the essence of being human.

I invite you to join me on this journey to discover what artificial intelligence and robotic technologies mean for humanity and to discuss how these advancements might shape society. Together, let us explore the boundaries of humanity's digital future.

Taner TAŞKIRAN

CONTENTS

1. INTRODUCTION

1.1. HUMANITY AT THE INTERSECTION OF ARTIFICIAL INTELLIGENCE AND HUMANOID ROBOTS

The history of humanity is a story of constant change and transformation. From the primitive caves where life began to the modern era shaped by groundbreaking discoveries, each period has brought its own revolution. The agricultural, industrial, and communication revolutions have paved the way for today's most defining shift: the age of artificial intelligence. This new era promises not just technological advancements but also a paradigm shift that challenges the very essence of what it means to be human.

Artificial intelligence, once confined to the realm of science fiction novels and movies, is now deeply integrated into almost every aspect of our lives. From healthcare to finance, education to manufacturing, AI has become a pivotal force. Unlike past technologies, AI stands out for its ability to analyze human behavior, process language, and even comprehend emotions, making it fundamentally different from anything humanity has encountered before.

The next step in this evolution is the physical embodiment of AI in the form of humanoid robots. These robots, designed to mimic human physical and mental capabilities, represent a technology that could potentially surpass its creators. They are not only designed to look human but also to think and make decisions like humans, heralding a future where robots coexist with humanity.

At the heart of this technological progress lies a profound question: Can human consciousness and personality be replicated in artificial intelligence? Our experiences, memories, emotions, and thoughts define who we are. If these can be transferred into an artificial system, does this signify a new beginning for humanity, or does it mark the loss of individuality?

The concept of digital immortality has sparked intense debate in this context. People wonder whether it is possible to transcend biological limits and continue living as a digital entity. This question is not merely technological; it lies at the intersection of philosophy, ethics, and society. After all, death is not just a biological end but a cornerstone that defines the meaning of life itself.

Artificial intelligence and humanoid robots may provide answers to these questions, but the journey involves more than technical solutions. It requires a re-examination of what it means to be human, how individuality is defined, and whether living within a robotic vessel truly captures the essence of humanity—or whether it is merely an imitation.

The integration of these technologies into our lives will also reshape societal and cultural dynamics. Human-robot interactions may bring about a new order in areas ranging from family structures to professional environments. The use of humanoid robots in education, healthcare, and elder care could simplify human life while simultaneously raising ethical concerns.

Another critical issue is the control and governance of these technologies. AI and humanoid robots have the potential to influence not only individual lives but also societal decision-making processes, and even the balance of power among nations. This is not just a technological advancement but also a redefinition of political and economic dynamics.

At this juncture, ethical questions become even more pressing. Can human consciousness be transferred into a machine without consent? Can a digitally replicated personality truly replace a living human? Most importantly, should such an entity be granted rights and responsibilities? These are some of the most complex and challenging dilemmas of the AI era.

While the boundaries of technology continue to expand, this expansion is not always beneficial to humanity. The potential risks associated with AI and humanoid robots highlight the importance of developing these technologies ethically and responsibly. If left unchecked, humanity may find itself trapped in a digital chaos where control is lost.

Ultimately, the intersection of artificial intelligence and humanoid robots holds immense potential for humanity. However, harnessing this potential requires a collective effort involving scientists, philosophers, policymakers, and society as a whole. As we strive to redefine the meaning of being human, preserving human values and responsibly shaping the future are tasks of paramount importance. This journey will test not only the limits of technology but also the boundaries of humanity itself.

1.2. FROM THE QUEST FOR IMMORTALITY TO DIGITAL IMMORTALITY

Throughout history, humanity has pursued the dream of immortality. This pursuit, rooted in ancient myths, religions, and literary works, reflects humanity's fear of death and its existential anxieties. Today, this dream has taken on a new dimension, evolving from fantasy to a plausible reality with the advancement of technology.

In mythological narratives, the secret of immortality was often held by gods or individuals with extraordinary powers. For instance, in Greek mythology, Prometheus bringing fire to humanity symbolizes the pursuit of knowledge and power beyond human reach. Similarly, in ancient Egyptian civilization, immortality was believed to be attainable by preserving the body, as evidenced by the mummification of pharaohs and the burial of their treasures.

Religions added a profound spiritual dimension to the quest for immortality. Concepts like heaven and hell introduced the idea of eternal life as a continuation of the soul's journey. The immortality of the soul underscored the belief that earthly life was transient, and eternal life awaited in another realm. However, with the advent of technology, this understanding has shifted toward a more tangible and scientific approach.

The Industrial Revolution and modern science began addressing immortality as a biological issue. Efforts to overcome the frailty of the human body and extend life focused on medical advancements, disease prevention, and longevity. Despite these efforts, death remains an insurmountable barrier that science has yet to overcome fully.

The emergence of digital technologies in the 20th century opened a new chapter in the quest for immortality. The development of computers, databases, and artificial intelligence introduced the idea that human life could continue in a digital form. People now seek ways to preserve their existence not just biologically but digitally.

The concept of digital immortality is based on transferring human personality traits, memories, and emotions into artificial intelligence. This process aims to create a digital copy of an individual, allowing their presence to persist even after physical death. This is no longer a mere science fiction fantasy but a scientifically explored possibility.

Artificial intelligence has become a central tool in realizing digital immortality. Its capabilities in natural language processing, emotional intelligence, and data analysis offer the potential to create human-like consciousness within a digital framework. By simulating human thoughts and behaviors, AI could enable the creation of a digital version of an individual.

Digital immortality is not just a technical endeavor; it raises profound ethical and philosophical questions. Does transferring a person's consciousness into a digital form truly ensure their continuity? Or is it merely an imitation? Can a digital copy fully replace the original human? These questions highlight both the potential and limitations of digital immortality.

This concept also has the potential to reshape societal dynamics. Digital immortality could strengthen or disrupt family bonds. For instance, people grieving the loss of loved ones might find solace in interacting with their digital counterparts, altering how we experience and process loss. However, this also raises questions about how humanity confronts and accepts the inevitability of death.

Economically and politically, digital immortality presents significant implications. Issues surrounding the ownership, rights, and responsibilities of digital entities would require new legal frameworks. Additionally, the societal roles of digitally immortalized individuals could redefine traditional notions of human life.

The greatest potential of this concept lies in its ability to challenge and redefine the meaning of being human. Can humanity transcend its biological existence and transition into a digital dimension? If so, this marks the beginning of a new era in human history. However, this process must proceed with caution, preserving human values and ethical boundaries.

Digital immortality also serves as a source of hope. By overcoming the finiteness imposed by death, humanity could find new meaning and continuity in life. This could revolutionize not only individuals' lives but also the collective memory of humanity itself.

Ultimately, digital immortality represents a technological transformation that seeks answers to one of the greatest questions in human history. This pursuit tests the boundaries not only of technology but also of humanity itself. Immortality is no longer a mere mythological dream; it is a possibility offered by the digital age. How this opportunity will be embraced and utilized is entirely up to us.

1.2.1. The Dream of Immortality Through History: A Journey from Mythology to Technology

The dream of immortality has manifested itself in various forms throughout history. This pursuit is a reflection of humanity's fear of death and its existential questions. For early humans, immortality represented a beacon of hope against the uncontrollable forces of nature. Struggling for survival, ancient societies expressed this aspiration through myths and legends. In Greek mythology, gods were synonymous with immortality, and mortals' greatest desire was to attain this divine power. Prometheus stealing fire from the gods to give it to humanity stands as one of the most enduring symbols of this dream.

Immortality found a place not only in mythological stories but also in religious beliefs. In ancient Egypt, it was believed that the soul was eternal, making the preservation of the body a matter of utmost importance. The mummification of pharaohs and the burial of wealth alongside them reflect this belief. In Hinduism and Buddhism, immortality is tied to the concept of reincarnation and the cycle of karma. These traditions viewed immortality not as a physical phenomenon but as the soul's perpetual existence.

Religion added a spiritual dimension to the idea of immortality, shifting the focus toward the afterlife. Concepts like heaven, hell, and eternal life shaped the belief that earthly existence was a temporary test, with true immortality awaiting in another realm. In this context, immortality was not an end in itself but a means of defining life's ultimate purpose. However, as modern science gained prominence, this understanding began to evolve toward a more tangible and physical pursuit of immortality.

The Industrial Revolution and scientific advancements introduced a new perspective on immortality. Humanity's focus shifted to overcoming the limitations of the body and extending life. Medical breakthroughs, disease prevention, and the discovery of life-extending treatments marked the early steps in this journey.

Research into slowing the aging process, genetic manipulation, and organ transplantation further reflected humanity's desire to transcend its biological boundaries. Yet, despite all progress, the inevitability of death remains an unsolved mystery.

The advent of digital technologies in the mid-20th century redefined the quest for immortality. The development of computers, data systems, and artificial intelligence introduced the possibility of extending human existence beyond biological limits. Today, people are increasingly drawn to the idea of preserving their lives in a digital format. The concept of digital immortality relies on transferring personal data, memories, and thoughts into artificial intelligence systems, ensuring the preservation of an individual's essence even after physical death.

Now, humanity's pursuit of immortality has evolved from mythology, religion, and biological research to artificial intelligence and digitalization. This journey is not merely a technological milestone but also a profound transformation that challenges humanity to rethink its existence and purpose. Immortality, once an unreachable fantasy, is becoming an attainable goal through science and technology. Yet, this ambition also brings ethical, societal, and philosophical challenges, setting the stage for some of the most significant debates in human history.

1.2.2. The Role of Artificial Intelligence and Humanoid Robots in Humanity's Search for Existence

The search for existence has been one of the most fundamental questions driving science, philosophy, and art throughout human history. Questions like "Who am I?", "Why am I here?", and "What happens after death?" reflect humanity's attempt to give meaning to its own existence. With the advancement of technology, these questions have taken on a new dimension, placing artificial intelligence and humanoid robots at the center of existential inquiry.

Artificial intelligence serves as a mirror in humanity's journey to understand itself. By mimicking human behavior, speaking our language, and even displaying emotional responses, AI offers humans a way to analyze their own nature more deeply. Through AI, humanity has the opportunity to model its own thought processes and emotional landscape, prompting a re-examination of what it truly means to be human.

Humanoid robots, on the other hand, give artificial intelligence a physical form. These robots, designed to replicate human shapes and movements, are built to establish deeper connections with people. This connection is not merely technical; it allows humans to see reflections of themselves in another entity. With their physical presence, humanoid robots expand humanity's perception of existence.

The role of AI and humanoid robots in the search for existence pushes the boundaries of human nature. Through these technologies, humanity imagines surpassing its own mental and physical limitations. Goals such as expanding memory capacity, halting aging, and continuing life as a digital entity after death reveal the transformative potential of these innovations.

At the heart of existential questions lies the concept of death. Humanity has built countless theories and civilizations around the question of what happens after death. However, AI and humanoid robots are challenging the idea that death is a definitive biological end. The possibility of transferring human consciousness into artificial forms supports the notion that existence can persist beyond physical life.

In this process, artificial intelligence attempts to model human emotions and thought processes. Understanding and mimicking human language allows AI to establish deeper communication with people. Technologies such as Natural Language Processing (NLP) enable AI to approximate human cognitive structures, creating pathways for transferring human thought into another entity.

The physical features of humanoid robots make it easier for humans to identify with them. Their facial expressions, movements, and tone of voice offer a more human-like experience by imitating human emotions. This interaction is not merely technological but also existential, as humans are naturally inclined to see their own existence reflected in these robots.

Another significant role of AI and humanoid robots is to serve humanity's desire to transcend physical and mental limitations. Humans turn to these technologies to enhance their capabilities and improve their lives. For instance, AI-powered prosthetics and humanoid robots in elder care are tools aimed at extending human life and improving quality of life.

These technologies also fuel human creativity and imagination. AI and humanoid robots push humans to question not only their existence but also their ability to create new forms of being. By creating entities that resemble themselves, humans explore their own capacity for creation, mirroring a godlike ability.

However, this process does not come without challenges. The role of AI and humanoid robots in the search for existence also raises profound ethical and philosophical questions. When humans transfer their existence into another form, can that form still be considered human? Can a digital copy truly replace the original person? These questions compel humanity to redefine the meaning of being human while questioning the limits of technology.

The relationship between humans and AI-powered humanoid robots also has the potential to transform societal structures. Interactions between humans and robots could create new norms in areas ranging from family dynamics to professional environments. For example, the use of humanoid robots in education and healthcare may lead humanity to redefine its traditional roles in these fields.

Another critical aspect is how these technologies could alter humanity's perception of death. Concepts such as digital immortality and AI-assisted memory replication might reshape how humans confront and process the idea of death. Death could shift from being an inevitable conclusion to a challenge that can be overcome.

In humanity's quest for existence, AI and humanoid robots are not just tools but also guides. Through these technologies, humans gain a deeper understanding of their own nature and limitations. However, ethical and responsible use of these technologies is crucial in this process.

At this point, humanity must ask itself: Do AI and humanoid robots make us more human, or do they cause us to lose our humanity? The potential offered by these technologies also requires the courage to seek answers to these profound questions.

Ultimately, AI and humanoid robots represent a significant turning point in humanity's search for existence. These technologies not only enhance human physical and mental capacities but also offer the courage to question the meaning of existence itself.

As humanity advances into a future shaped by these innovations, it carries the responsibility of preserving its values and purpose.

1.3. WHAT IS THE TRANSFERENCE OF HUMAN CONSCIOUSNESS TO AI AND ROBOTIC SYSTEMS?

The transference of human consciousness to artificial intelligence (AI) and robotic systems refers to the process of digitally replicating an individual's personality traits, thought processes, memories, and emotions. This concept involves recreating human consciousness within an artificial system, enabling the individual's existence to persist in a new, non-biological form, even after death. Also referred to as digital immortality, this idea represents a groundbreaking effort by science and technology to redefine the essence of human existence.

This concept is not merely a technical endeavor but also addresses one of humanity's oldest and most profound questions: Can human existence transcend the biological body? The idea of continuing one's existence as a digital entity presents a vision of a world where biological limitations are overcome. However, this process raises not only technological challenges but also ethical, philosophical, and societal questions.

The process of transference aims to create a digital representation of an individual. This digital entity replicates the person's communication style, decision-making processes, and even emotional responses. To achieve this, vast amounts of personal data—such as social media posts, emails, and videos—are collected and analyzed to construct a personality map. This map serves as the foundation for understanding and replicating the individual's behavior and thought patterns.

Robotic systems add a physical dimension to this digital representation. Humanoid robots act as physical vessels for AI-driven consciousness, allowing the digital entity to exist in a tangible, interactive form. These robots can simulate not only cognitive functions but also physical gestures and social interactions, enabling a digital presence to manifest in the real world.

At the core of this technology lies the idea that human consciousness can be recreated within an artificial system. While consciousness remains one of the most complex and unresolved topics in neuroscience and AI, researchers argue that human cognitive processes can be mimicked through algorithms and data. This involves translating the neural connections and cognitive functions of the human brain into AI models.

The transference process must encompass not only thought patterns but also emotional responses and empathy. At the heart of being human lies the ability to form emotional connections and respond to others on an emotional level. Imparting emotional intelligence to AI is one of the most intricate and critical aspects of this process.

Robotic systems further enhance this process by providing a tangible form for digital consciousness. A digital copy of an individual could inhabit a humanoid robot, possessing not only the person's thoughts and emotions but also their physical expressions and movements. For instance, a humanoid robot could mimic a person's characteristic facial expressions, gestures, and even vocal tone, making the replication more authentic and relatable.

The potential benefits of this technology are immense. Digitally replicated individuals could make significant contributions in fields such as education, healthcare, and consulting. For example, the expertise of a renowned doctor could be preserved and utilized by AI systems to continue providing medical insights even after their passing. This would create an invaluable legacy of knowledge for humanity.

However, this process also raises serious ethical concerns. Can an individual's consciousness be transferred without their consent? Would a digital replica possess the same rights as the original person? These questions are not just about individual ethics but also about societal norms and the need for new legal frameworks to address the implications of such technologies.

The process of digital transference also has the potential to alter humanity's perception of death. Throughout history, death has been seen as the inevitable end of life. However, the concept of digital immortality challenges this notion, suggesting that death could be an obstacle to overcome. People could continue interacting with their loved ones through digital entities, redefining how society processes and confronts loss.

This technology also redefines human-machine relationships. The integration of digital replicas and humanoid robots into society could create new dynamics, influencing family bonds and professional environments. For instance, humanoid robots in education and healthcare could lead humanity to rethink its traditional roles in these sectors.

The idea of transference to AI and robotic systems also has profound implications for human creativity and imagination. By creating entities that resemble themselves, humans explore their capacity for creation and challenge the boundaries of what it means to exist. This process reflects humanity's desire to transcend its own limitations and create new forms of being.

Yet, the risks of this technology must not be overlooked. The misuse of digital replicas could violate individual privacy or exacerbate societal inequalities. Developing this technology ethically and responsibly is essential to mitigate these potential dangers.

In essence, the transference of human consciousness to AI and robotic systems represents both a scientific and philosophical revolution. While it holds the promise of transcending humanity's biological boundaries, it also demands a redefinition of what it means to be human. The future impact of this technology could mark the beginning of a new era for humanity.

The concept of digital immortality and the advent of humanoid robots create a new reality that challenges the boundaries of both technology and humanity. The effort to recreate human existence in an artificial form is both awe-inspiring and deeply thought-provoking, signaling a transformation that could redefine the human experience.

1.3.1. Definition and Scope of the Concept

The transference of human consciousness to artificial intelligence (AI) and robotic systems refers to the process of digitally replicating an individual's mental, emotional, and behavioral characteristics. This involves recreating human consciousness through AI algorithms, allowing the individual to continue existing in a digital format or within a humanoid robot. Often referred to as digital immortality, this concept is rooted in the idea of extending human life beyond biological boundaries.

At its core, this concept challenges humanity to redefine what it means to exist. Can human consciousness, memories, and emotions be transferred to an artificial system? If so, does this transfer ensure the continuity of the individual's identity? The concept not only aims to address these questions but also opens up philosophical debates that transcend technology.

The process begins by analyzing all the data a person generates throughout their life. Social media posts, digital communications, biometric data, and other behavioral traces are used to create a personality map. This map serves as a foundation for understanding the individual's thought patterns, emotional responses, and social interactions.

This data is then integrated into AI algorithms to construct a digital model of the individual. The model simulates the person's personality traits, decision-making processes, and emotional states. For example, AI can predict how the individual might respond in specific scenarios and replicate those responses in the digital entity.

Robotic systems take this digital model and give it a physical form. Humanoid robots act as physical vessels for AI-driven consciousness. These robots can mimic an individual's facial expressions, movements, and tone of voice, making the digital entity a tangible presence in the real world.

The concept's scope extends beyond merely copying consciousness. It encompasses societal, ethical, and legal dimensions as well. For instance, can a digital entity possess rights and responsibilities? Could a digital entity inherit property or be held accountable for actions? These questions expand the concept's boundaries, sparking deeper discussions.

One crucial aspect of the process is the transference of emotional intelligence. Being human is not solely about rational thought; emotions play a fundamental role. Teaching AI to replicate emotions such as love, fear, and empathy is one of the most complex and controversial aspects of this concept.

On a societal level, the concept has the potential to bring about significant changes. Digital immortality could transform the way people experience grief. Those who have lost loved ones could interact with their digital representations, potentially reshaping the mourning process. However, this also raises questions about the nature of death and its impact on human life.

The concept could also have far-reaching economic and political implications. The use of digital entities as economic resources could redefine labor markets and production processes. Additionally, the potential role of digital entities in political decision-making might influence future governance models.

The transference process also enhances human creativity and imagination. By creating entities that resemble themselves, humans explore their godlike potential for creation. This is not just a technological achievement but also a redefinition of human nature and its boundaries.

However, the concept also brings potential risks. Misuse of digital entities could infringe on individuals' privacy. Moreover, such technologies could deepen societal inequalities. For example, a world where only the wealthy have access to digital immortality could exacerbate economic and social divides.

The scope of this technology also challenges humanity's perception of death. Throughout history, death has been regarded as an inevitable end. Digital immortality, however, suggests that death may not be a finality but a challenge that can be overcome. This could fundamentally alter humanity's understanding of existence.

The ethical dimensions of the concept are critical. Can a digital copy have the same rights and responsibilities as the original individual? Can it fully represent the person, or is it merely an imitation? These questions are essential for understanding the potential and limitations of this concept.

Another aspect is the need for legal frameworks. The legal status, rights, and responsibilities of digital entities must be clearly defined. For instance, if a digital entity commits a crime, who would be held accountable? Such questions necessitate the redesign of future legal systems.

Ultimately, the transference of human consciousness to AI and robotic systems represents a technological revolution. Yet, it is not just a technical achievement—it is a transformation that redefines the meaning of being human. While it holds the potential to transcend biological boundaries, it also carries ethical and societal responsibilities.

The concept's scope includes the recreation of humanity's physical, mental, and emotional existence. However, this effort must be balanced with the responsibility to preserve human values and meaning. The ethical and responsible use of technology is vital to the successful implementation of this concept.

In conclusion, the transference of human consciousness to AI and robotic systems is not merely a scientific milestone but a journey that tests the boundaries of humanity itself. This journey marks the beginning of a new era for humanity and requires the courage to question the meaning of existence anew.

1.3.2. Technological, Ethical, and Philosophical Dimensions

The concept of transferring human consciousness to artificial intelligence (AI) and robotic systems represents not only a scientific revolution but also a profound area of debate. This idea pushes the boundaries of technology while compelling humanity to reevaluate its ethical and philosophical values. The process encompasses three interconnected dimensions: technological, ethical, and philosophical.

From a technological perspective, transferring human consciousness to AI is an extraordinary engineering challenge. It involves mimicking the neural networks and cognitive processes of the human brain using complex algorithms and massive datasets. Creating a simulation of the brain requires not just storing information but also processing it dynamically. This is one of the most intricate tasks AI technology has ever undertaken.

The inclusion of robotic systems adds a physical aspect to this process. When a person's digital copy is embedded into a humanoid robot, it becomes not only a mental but also a physical entity. This allows the replication of not just speech patterns and decision-making processes but also facial expressions, movements, and vocal tones.

However, technological achievements bring with them critical ethical questions. Can human consciousness be transferred to an artificial system without the individual's consent? How can privacy be ensured during the replication process? More importantly, can these digital entities fully represent the original individual, or are they merely imitations? These questions challenge the ethical boundaries of technology.

One significant ethical concern involves the rights and responsibilities of digital entities. Can a digital copy have rights similar to a human? For example, could a digital entity inherit property or be held legally accountable? Such scenarios highlight the need for an entirely new legal framework for humanity.

Additionally, the societal impact of digital immortality demands ethical scrutiny. If this technology becomes accessible only to a wealthy minority, it could exacerbate social inequalities. This would create not only economic but also social and cultural issues. Ensuring fair access to such technologies lies at the heart of ethical debates.

From a philosophical standpoint, the meaning of being human becomes the central topic of discussion. Can a digital copy of a person truly replace the original? If it can, how does this redefine the essence of being human? What would a digitally immortal humanity signify for human history? These questions help us understand the boundaries and potential of digital immortality.

Another critical philosophical issue is the definition of consciousness. Is consciousness merely a physical activity of the brain, or does it have a spiritual and metaphysical dimension? If it is purely physical, then it might be replicable in artificial systems. However, if consciousness transcends the physical world, its complete replication in AI may remain unattainable.

These discussions also require a reexamination of the concept of death. Digital immortality challenges the idea of death as a definitive end, suggesting that it could be an obstacle to overcome. However, how would this alter the psychological and societal effects of death? If people continue to exist as digital entities, the meaning of confronting death could fundamentally change.

Technology's effort to address such existential questions forces humanity to redefine itself. By recreating human existence in an artificial system, humanity dares to transcend its limitations. However, this ambition also comes with profound responsibility. Humanity must use this technology ethically and responsibly.

Digital immortality has the potential to bring about not only individual transformation but also societal transformation. Human-robot interactions could create new norms in areas ranging from family dynamics to professional environments. For instance, the use of digital entities in education and healthcare could reshape societal structures.

This transformation could also impact human emotional and social connections. While a digital entity allows loved ones to interact with a recreated individual, how authentic would these interactions feel? Can bonds formed with digital entities replace human-to-human connections? These questions deepen the philosophical and ethical dimensions of the technology.

Ultimately, the technological, ethical, and philosophical dimensions cannot be viewed in isolation. Together, they form a holistic framework that challenges humanity to redefine the meaning of existence. While technology offers the opportunity to transcend limitations, it also demands a careful examination of what lies beyond those boundaries.

For this process to succeed, humanity must safeguard its ethical values and societal responsibilities. Technology is merely a tool; how it is used will shape the future of humanity.

Digital immortality and AI represent one of the most significant transformations in human history. However, this transformation is not just a technological achievement but also a profound philosophical and ethical test. Humanity must understand and guide this technology responsibly to pass this test.

In conclusion, the technological, ethical, and philosophical dimensions together create a comprehensive narrative of humanity's attempt to recreate itself in artificial systems. This effort challenges not only the limits of technology but also the values and meaning of humanity, marking the beginning of a new era.

1.4. PURPOSE AND METHODOLOGY OF THE BOOK

The primary aim of this book is to comprehensively explore the concept of transferring human consciousness to artificial intelligence (AI) and robotic systems. It delves into the technological, ethical, and philosophical dimensions of this process, examining the challenges it presents and offering insights into its future implications. At its core, the book seeks to understand how the age-old human aspiration for immortality has been transformed in the digital era.

This book is not merely a compilation of technological advancements; it also aims to redefine the essence of being human, question the nature of consciousness, and analyze the profound impact of this concept on humanity. While digital immortality stems from scientific curiosity, it holds the potential to generate far-reaching consequences on both societal and individual levels. Another objective of this work is to highlight these consequences and provide humanity with a roadmap for navigating them.

Digital immortality is not solely about extending individual lives; it is also a means of preserving human knowledge for future generations. In this context, the book emphasizes the positive impacts of digital replication technologies on individuals and society while also addressing potential risks. Issues such as social inequality, privacy breaches, and ethical dilemmas are critically examined to provide a balanced perspective.

The methodological approach of the book is interdisciplinary, drawing from fields such as artificial intelligence, robotics, neuroscience, ethics, law, and philosophy. This framework allows for a multidimensional analysis of the topic, ensuring not only an understanding of technological advancements but also their profound societal implications.

Based on scientific data and contemporary research, each chapter offers concrete examples and real-world applications of the concept. This approach enables readers to not only engage with theoretical discussions but also understand how these technologies could influence daily life.

The book employs foresight and scenario analysis methods to present various perspectives on the future. Speculative but scientifically grounded projections explore how digital immortality and humanoid robots might shape the future of humanity. Utopian and dystopian scenarios are presented to encourage readers to critically evaluate these technologies.

Another method employed in this work involves exploring the concept through personal narratives. By examining the experiences of individuals undergoing digital replication, the book investigates the personal and emotional effects of these technologies. Such examples highlight that this is not merely a scientific advancement but also a phenomenon at the heart of human life.

The book discusses not only the present but also the future. It examines the long-term impact of digital immortality on future generations, situating this technological transformation within the broader context of human history. Projections are made about how these technologies could redefine humanity's self-perception and transform societal structures.

Readers are encouraged to contemplate a fundamental question: Is digital immortality a salvation for humanity, or does it pose a threat to identity? To answer this, the book emphasizes the importance of considering not only technological progress but also its ethical and philosophical dimensions.

Ethical discussions form a central part of this book. Analyses of the rights, responsibilities, and societal roles of digital replicas help define the boundaries of technology. Additionally, issues such as ensuring consent and protecting privacy during the replication process are explored in detail.

The lack of legal frameworks and the challenges posed by this technology are another focus of the book's methodology. It examines the necessity of creating legal structures for digital replicas in the future and explores how the rights of individuals can be protected during this process. This discussion seeks to identify pathways for creating a society that harmonizes with technology.

The book's purpose is not only to inform but also to provoke thought and inspire action. Readers are prompted to consider how humanity will shape and adapt to this technological transformation and what role they will play in it.

Methodologically, the book adopts an analytical approach. It begins with a broad overview of the subject before delving into more specific and detailed aspects. This method helps readers develop a comprehensive understanding of the topic.

A comparative analysis approach is also employed. By examining similarities and differences between past technological revolutions and digital immortality, the book identifies the place of this transformation in human history.

In conclusion, this book aims to serve as a guide in humanity's effort to redefine itself. Positioned at the intersection of technology, ethics, and philosophy, the subject is not just a scientific discussion but also a new beginning for humanity. This book seeks to contribute to understanding and shaping this new beginning.

1.4.1. Fundamental Questions: Can Human Consciousness Be Transferred to AI and Robots?

Human consciousness has long been one of the greatest mysteries explored by philosophers, scientists, and artists throughout history. The nature, scope, and limits of consciousness have now taken on a new dimension with the rise of artificial intelligence (AI) and robotics. Can human consciousness truly be transferred to an artificial system? Answering this question has the potential not only to push the boundaries of technology but also to redefine the very essence of being human.

The idea of transferring consciousness first requires a clear definition of what consciousness is. It is often described as a state of self-awareness that includes thoughts, emotions, memories, and decision-making processes. However, this definition remains elusive, as consciousness can be seen as both a physical and metaphysical phenomenon. This complexity makes the task of transferring consciousness to an artificial system even more challenging

AI technologies hold the potential to model various aspects of human consciousness. Techniques such as Natural Language Processing (NLP), deep learning algorithms, and big data analysis are used to understand and simulate human thought processes and behaviors. However, these technologies primarily aim to mimic intelligence and decision-making, not consciousness itself.

To transfer consciousness, the neural networks and cognitive processes of the human brain must be fully mapped. Advances in neuroscience have identified specific brain regions associated with functions such as memory, emotions, and motor skills. However, these discoveries are not enough to capture the full complexity of consciousness.

Another critical question is whether consciousness is purely a physical phenomenon. If it is merely the result of neural connections and electrical activity, then it might be possible to replicate it in artificial systems. However, if consciousness has a non-physical or metaphysical dimension, its replication in artificial systems could be impossible. This raises the question of whether consciousness has a spiritual or non-material component.

The concept of transferring consciousness also poses significant ethical dilemmas. Can a person's consciousness be transferred without their consent? If consciousness is transferred to an artificial system, can it fully represent the original individual? Or is it merely an imitation? These questions highlight the ethical challenges surrounding the process of replication.

Robotic systems offer a physical form for artificial consciousness. A person's digital consciousness could be embodied in a humanoid robot. However, would this robot be seen as merely a physical simulation, or could it be perceived as a true individual? Could its emotional and social interactions enable it to be accepted as human-like?

Emotional intelligence is a crucial component of consciousness. Replicating not only thought processes but also emotional responses is essential for fully recreating consciousness. But are emotions simply neural activities, or do they represent a deeper aspect of human existence?

Another fundamental question is what it truly means to transfer consciousness. If a person's consciousness is transferred to an artificial system, does this mean the individual continues to exist after death? Or does it merely create a copy of the person while the original ceases to exist? The answer to this question forms the foundation of the concept of digital immortality.

The idea of transferring consciousness could also lead to profound societal changes. The integration of digital copies into society could create new norms, affecting everything from family bonds to workplace dynamics. Human-robot relationships might redefine societal structures and interactions.

While technological advancements may make consciousness transfer feasible, the process is still constrained by unresolved ethical and philosophical questions. For example, could a digital copy have the same rights as the original individual? Can it fully retain the person's memories and experiences? Or would it be nothing more than a database of information?

The process of transferring consciousness also has the potential to reshape the concept of death. Digital immortality suggests that death is not a final end but rather an obstacle that can be overcome. However, how would this change the psychological and societal impacts of death? Could people experience the process of grieving and loss in entirely new ways?

Ultimately, the idea of transferring human consciousness to AI and robots is both a scientific and philosophical challenge. This process forces us to not only push the boundaries of technology but also to rethink the meaning of humanity itself.

Answering these questions requires the involvement of not just scientists but also philosophers, ethicists, and society as a whole. Humanity must grapple with its own values and limitations while developing this technology.

If human consciousness can truly be transferred to an artificial system, it could mark the beginning of a new era for humanity. However, the ethical and responsible development of this technology is crucial to its success.

These questions are not just a scientific inquiry but also a profound existential exploration for humanity. Can humanity transcend its own limitations by transferring consciousness? If so, how might this reshape the course of human history?

In conclusion, the question of whether human consciousness can be transferred to AI and robots lies at the intersection of technology, ethics, and philosophy. This process represents both a tremendous opportunity and a profound responsibility for humanity.

1.4.2. The Interdisciplinary Approach and Scope of the Book

This book adopts an interdisciplinary approach to deeply examine the concept of transferring human consciousness to artificial intelligence (AI) and robotic systems. The complexity and multidimensionality of the subject cannot be addressed through a single field of study. As such, the book integrates contributions from AI, robotics, neuroscience, ethics, law, sociology, philosophy, and psychology to provide a comprehensive exploration

AI technologies form the foundation for modeling and simulating human consciousness. Techniques such as deep learning algorithms, big data analysis, and natural language processing (NLP) play a critical role in understanding human thought processes and behaviors. The book analyzes the potential and limitations of these technologies in replicating consciousness.

Neuroscience is pivotal for understanding the biological basis of consciousness. Mapping the neural networks and cognitive processes of the human brain provides essential insights for recreating consciousness in artificial systems. The book highlights the latest developments in neuroscience and their connections to AI, offering an explanation of the biological foundations of consciousness.

Robotics provides the physical embodiment of consciousness. Humanoid robots, integrated with AI, allow for the simulation of human thought and behavior in a physical environment. The book explores the potential of robotic systems to represent human consciousness and discusses the societal implications of this technology.

Ethics is another central discipline addressed in the book. The replication of human consciousness raises numerous ethical questions, including individual rights, privacy, consent, and the rights of digital entities. The book examines these ethical dilemmas, emphasizing that the replication of consciousness has profound moral implications alongside its technological possibilities.

Law plays a crucial role in the integration of digital entities into society. Technologies like digital immortality and consciousness replication require new legal frameworks that go beyond existing systems. The book analyzes the legal challenges posed by digital entities, including their rights, responsibilities, and societal roles.

Sociology is essential for understanding the societal impact of these technologies. The integration of digital replicas into societal norms, family structures, and human relationships is a core topic of the book. It also presents projections on how human-robot relationships might shape new societal dynamics.

Philosophy addresses fundamental questions about the definition and nature of consciousness. Is consciousness merely a physical phenomenon, or does it possess a metaphysical dimension? This question shapes the book's philosophical discussions, which also explore the meaning of being human, identity, and existence.

Psychology focuses on the emotional and cognitive aspects of consciousness. The book examines whether human emotions and thoughts can be transferred to artificial systems and how this might impact an individual's sense of self.

By combining these disciplines, the book aims not only to provide an academic perspective but also to raise awareness about the opportunities and risks associated with these advancements. The contributions from each field enable a more holistic understanding of the subject.

The scope of the book extends from the technical details of technological developments to their societal, ethical, and individual consequences. The subject is treated not just as a scientific discussion but also as an existential inquiry for humanity.

Additionally, the book employs scenario analysis to explore the potential future impacts of digital immortality. By presenting utopian and dystopian perspectives, it offers projections on how these technologies could shape the future of humanity.

In conclusion, this book serves as an interdisciplinary guide to understanding humanity's effort to recreate itself in artificial systems. Positioned at the intersection of technology, ethics, and philosophy, the subject challenges not only the boundaries of human capability but also the courage to redefine what it means to be human.

2. HUMAN PERSONALITY AND CONSCIOUSNESS: SCIENTIFIC AND TECHNOLOGICAL FOUNDATION

Human personality and consciousness are among the most complex and researched aspects of existence. Consciousness is the state of self-awareness, encompassing thoughts, emotions, and memories, while personality refers to the enduring traits that shape an individual's behavior, attitudes, and reactions. These two concepts lie at the heart of understanding humanity, both biologically and technologically.

The scientific foundations of consciousness are deeply rooted in neuroscience. The neural networks and neurons in the human brain are fundamental to conscious experiences. Specific brain regions, particularly the prefrontal cortex and limbic system, are directly linked to thought processes, emotions, and decision-making. However, a definitive explanation of how consciousness arises remains elusive, making it one of the greatest mysteries in science.

Personality is shaped by a combination of genetic and environmental factors. While genetics influence specific personality traits, environmental elements play a critical role in their development. Psychological research has developed models like the Big Five personality traits to measure and categorize personality. These models provide a basis for technological systems to understand and replicate human personality.

Artificial intelligence (AI) serves as a powerful tool for understanding and simulating human consciousness and personality. Big data analytics and deep learning algorithms are used to study human behavior and thought processes. For instance, natural language processing (NLP) techniques analyze language use to model an individual's thought patterns and emotional states.

Neural networks enable AI systems to mimic the functioning of the human brain. These networks, inspired by the workings of biological neurons, can simulate human thought processes. However, the ability of artificial systems to develop true consciousness remains a topic of debate, pushing the boundaries of technology and sparking philosophical discussions.

Robotic systems allow for the physical embodiment of human personality and consciousness. Humanoid robots can replicate an individual's behaviors, gestures, and emotional responses, offering an experience closer to human interaction. This serves as a critical tool for understanding how consciousness and personality can be materialized in digital systems.

Despite advancements, the question of whether consciousness and personality can be fully replicated remains unanswered. Is consciousness purely a physical phenomenon, or does it have a metaphysical dimension? If it is entirely biological, it may be possible to recreate these processes in artificial systems. However, if consciousness includes a non-material component, replication may be impossible.

Beyond scientific foundations, the societal and ethical implications of transferring consciousness and personality to digital systems must also be considered. This process could affect individuals' privacy, identity, and roles within society. The rights and responsibilities of digital replicas, in particular, are critical topics in legal and ethical debates.

AI and robotic technologies hold the potential to recreate human personality and consciousness, but the limits of this process remain uncertain. Without a complete understanding of consciousness, achieving its full transfer to artificial systems is challenging. This uncertainty underscores the need for continued scientific research and ethical reflection.

Human personality and consciousness have become not only tools for technological systems but also their primary objectives. This represents one of the most significant transformations in human history. However, this transformation must be seen not just as a scientific achievement but as a process of redefining humanity's existence and values.

In conclusion, the scientific and technological foundations of human personality and consciousness are being reshaped by advancements in AI and robotics. For this process to succeed, collaboration between science, ethics, and philosophy is essential. This is not merely a technological revolution but also an existential exploration for humanity.

2.1. PERSONALITY AND CONSCIOUSNESS: THE FOUNDATION OF BEING HUMAN

Personality and consciousness are the fundamental building blocks of what it means to be human. These two concepts shape an individual's perception of themselves and their surroundings, their social interactions, and their sense of purpose. Consciousness is the awareness of thoughts, emotions, and memories, while personality defines the consistent patterns of attitudes and behaviors that make each individual unique. Together, they enable humans to transcend their biological existence.

Consciousness allows humans to make sense of their existence. It is at the core of cognitive processes such as thinking, feeling, and decision-making. Through consciousness, individuals learn from past experiences, analyze their present circumstances, and plan for the future. It is not merely the sum of individual experiences; it is also the foundation of how humans relate to their environment.

Personality, on the other hand, governs behavior and distinguishes one individual from another. It is shaped by a combination of genetic predispositions and environmental influences. Personality emerges from the interplay of emotional, cognitive, and social factors, creating a unique identity for each individual and contributing to the diversity of society.

When combined, consciousness and personality form the holistic essence of being human. Consciousness enables individuals to understand their thoughts and feelings, while personality translates these into actions. Together, they create a dynamic process through which humans interact with themselves and the world around them.

These qualities are not only the foundation of individual existence but also the bedrock of social structures. Consciousness and personality enable empathy, cooperation, and the strengthening of social bonds. In this way, the capacity for self-awareness and self-expression directly influences the functioning of societies.

Today, artificial intelligence and robotics hold the potential to imitate consciousness and personality. However, these attempts fall short of capturing the full complexity of human nature. Consciousness and personality are the result of the intricate interplay between biological, emotional, and social elements, making it difficult to fully replicate them in artificial systems.

The centrality of consciousness and personality to the human experience also makes them one of humanity's greatest responsibilities. Preserving and nurturing these qualities requires adherence to ethical and moral values. Consciousness and personality are not merely individual traits but also part of the shared heritage of humanity.

Technological advancements may lead to a redefinition of consciousness and personality. However, for this transformation to succeed, scientific research must be accompanied by ethical and philosophical discussions. Attempting to recreate these fundamental aspects in artificial systems without a deep understanding of their essence risks losing the very core of human nature.

In conclusion, personality and consciousness are the indispensable foundations of being human. They not only help individuals understand themselves but also strengthen their connection to society and the world. Humanity must strive to understand and protect these foundations through both scientific and humanistic efforts.

2.1.1. Definitions of Personality and Consciousness in Psychology

Psychology views personality and consciousness as fundamental concepts for understanding human nature. These two constructs play a decisive role in shaping how individuals perceive and express themselves, their environment, and their lives. Personality refers to the consistent patterns of behavior and characteristic traits of an individual, while consciousness encompasses the state of awareness, subjective experiences, and self-reflection.

Personality is defined as the enduring patterns of thoughts, feelings, and behaviors exhibited consistently by an individual over time. In psychology, personality is considered a combination of genetic predispositions, environmental influences, and life experiences. It is one of the core elements that distinguish individuals and determines how they respond to their surroundings.

Early psychologists such as Sigmund Freud described personality as a dynamic interplay between conscious and unconscious processes. Freud's psychoanalytic approach conceptualized personality through three components: the id, ego, and superego. This model provided a framework for understanding how both conscious and unconscious elements influence behavior.

Modern approaches examine personality through constructs like the Five-Factor Model (Big Five). This model categorizes personality into five broad dimensions: openness, conscientiousness, extraversion, agreeableness, and neuroticism. These dimensions serve as a comprehensive basis for predicting and understanding individual behavior.

Consciousness, on the other hand, is defined as a state of subjective awareness. In psychology, consciousness enables individuals to understand their own thoughts, feelings, and surroundings. It allows for the exploration of one's inner world and the establishment of meaningful connections with the external world.

William James famously described consciousness as a "stream of thought," emphasizing its continuous and ever-changing nature. According to James, consciousness is a process that integrates experiences over time, creating a sense of coherence and unity. This perspective highlights the dynamic and ongoing nature of consciousness.

In modern psychology, consciousness is often examined through two main dimensions: content and level. The content of consciousness includes thoughts, emotions, and memories of which an individual is aware. The level of consciousness refers to aspects such as wakefulness, depth of awareness, and states of alertness.

Neuroscience plays a significant role in the study of consciousness. Research has identified specific regions of the brain associated with conscious experiences. For instance, the prefrontal cortex supports thinking and decision-making, while the limbic system is linked to emotional experiences. These discoveries provide insights into the biological foundations of consciousness.

In psychology, personality and consciousness are critical to the formation of identity. While personality shapes how individuals react to the external world and interact with others, consciousness enables them to develop a deeper understanding of their own existence. Together, these two constructs form an integral part of the human experience.

Personality and consciousness help individuals make sense of themselves and their environment. Personality determines how individuals behave in social contexts, while consciousness allows them to reflect on the underlying reasons for their behaviors. The integration of these two concepts enables a holistic understanding of human behavior.

The study of personality and consciousness in psychology has implications not only at the individual level but also at the societal level. These concepts facilitate the formation of social bonds, cooperation, and empathy among individuals. This makes them essential for both individual and collective well-being.

In conclusion, personality and consciousness are indispensable constructs in psychology for understanding human nature. Exploring these concepts not only explains individual behavior but also deepens our understanding of the relationship between humans and their world.

2.1.2. The Scientific Basis of Emotions, Thoughts, and Behaviors

Emotions, thoughts, and behaviors are fundamental elements that shape human interaction with the environment and provide meaning to life experiences. Psychology, neuroscience, and behavioral sciences have developed comprehensive theories and methods to understand and explain these three essential processes. They are influenced by a combination of biological and environmental factors.

Emotions are complex psychological and physiological responses to internal and external stimuli. Neuroscience focuses on the limbic system in the brain to understand the foundation of emotions. The amygdala, a key component of the limbic system, plays a critical role in processing emotions such as fear and anger.

Meanwhile, the prefrontal cortex regulates and controls emotional responses.

Thoughts represent the cognitive processes through which the human mind processes information. Scientists have discovered that thoughts are transmitted via neural networks in the brain, carried out through electrochemical signals. The prefrontal cortex is central to higher-order cognitive processes such as reasoning, problem-solving, and decision-making. It is responsible for organizing and planning thoughts.

Emotions directly influence thoughts and, consequently, behaviors. For instance, when a person feels threatened, the emotion of fear focuses their thoughts on escaping danger, triggering avoidance behavior. The connection between these three processes enables individuals to adapt to their environment and survive.

Behaviors are defined as the tangible actions through which individuals express their emotions and thoughts. The scientific basis of behavior lies in both internal motivations and external stimuli. For example, the dopamine system plays a significant role in motivating behavior by influencing reward mechanisms.

In addition to biological foundations, environmental factors also shape emotions, thoughts, and behaviors. Childhood experiences play a critical role in emotional and cognitive development. Furthermore, social norms and cultural values influence how individuals think, feel, and behave.

The relationship between emotions, thoughts, and behaviors is also crucial in learning processes. Behavioral psychology explores how rewards and punishments shape behavior, while cognitive psychology focuses on the role of thoughts and cognitive structures in learning. Both perspectives provide insights into how individuals interact with their environment.

The complex interaction between emotions, thoughts, and behaviors is evident in areas such as stress and mental health. For instance, chronic stress can negatively impact emotional and cognitive processes, leading to adverse behavioral outcomes. This highlights the need for collaboration between neuroscience and psychology to develop strategies for maintaining mental well-being.

Technological advancements have provided new tools for studying the scientific basis of emotions, thoughts, and behaviors. Brain imaging techniques, such as fMRI and EEG, allow researchers to observe brain activity and understand how emotional and cognitive processes function. These tools have advanced our understanding of the biological underpinnings of these processes.

Emotions and thoughts are not only significant at the individual level but also play a crucial role in the social context. Empathy, cooperation, and social bonds arise as a result of emotional and cognitive processes. Understanding these processes is essential for comprehending human behavior on both individual and societal levels.

The scientific basis of emotions, thoughts, and behaviors also inspires the development of artificial intelligence and robotic systems. These systems aim to replicate emotional intelligence and cognitive processes to create human-like interactions. However, they are still limited in fully capturing the depth and complexity of human emotions and thoughts.

In conclusion, emotions, thoughts, and behaviors are the cornerstone of human nature, shaped by a combination of biological, psychological, and environmental factors. Understanding their scientific basis is critical not only for interpreting human behavior but also for improving mental health and strengthening the relationship between technology and humanity.

The intricate interplay between emotions, thoughts, and behaviors lies at the heart of human interaction with the environment. A deeper understanding of these processes will contribute to guiding both individuals and societies toward a better future.

2.2. MODELS OF PERSONALITY AND CONSCIOUSNESS

Personality and consciousness are two fundamental components of human psychology, and various theoretical models have been developed to understand these concepts. These models help individuals comprehend themselves and their relationships with others. Positioned at the intersection of psychology, neuroscience, and philosophy, models of personality and consciousness aim to explain, predict, and shape human behavior.

Personality models focus on understanding the underlying structures and tendencies behind individuals' behaviors. The Five-Factor Model (Big Five) is one of the most widely accepted frameworks in modern psychology. It defines personality across five key dimensions: openness, conscientiousness, extraversion, agreeableness, and neuroticism. These dimensions provide insights into individuals' behaviors and social interactions.

Another significant personality model is Carl Jung's theory of psychological types. Jung proposed that individuals could be categorized as introverted or extroverted and could differ in their preferences for perceiving, thinking, and feeling. This theory laid the groundwork for tools like the Myers-Briggs Type Indicator

(MBTI), a popular test used to identify personality types and provide guidance based on these classifications.

Consciousness models, on the other hand, focus on understanding subjective experiences and levels of awareness. Sigmund Freud's model of consciousness consists of three levels: the conscious, the subconscious, and the unconscious. This framework seeks to explain how thoughts and emotions outside of conscious awareness can influence behavior.

William James's model of consciousness, which describes it as a "stream of thought," emphasizes its continuous and dynamic nature. James highlighted how conscious experiences flow and connect over time, creating a sense of unity and coherence. This model underscores the integrative and meaningful aspects of consciousness.

Modern neuroscience has developed models to understand the biological foundations of consciousness. For example, the Global Workspace Theory suggests that consciousness arises from the sharing and integration of information across different regions of the brain. This model attempts to explain how complex information processing leads to conscious awareness.

Models of personality and consciousness have significance not only at the individual level but also at the societal level. Personality models help explain how individuals interact in social contexts, while consciousness models play a critical role in understanding self-awareness and empathy. These frameworks provide powerful tools for examining human behavior in both individual and collective contexts.

In conclusion, models of personality and consciousness enable us to understand the mechanisms underlying human behavior and use this knowledge to contribute to the development of individuals and societies. By exploring these models, we gain a deeper understanding of the fundamental dynamics of being human.

2.2.1. The Five-Factor Model (Big Five)

The Five-Factor Model, also known as the Big Five, is one of the most widely accepted frameworks for understanding personality in modern psychology. This model categorizes personality into five broad dimensions: openness, conscientiousness, extraversion, agreeableness, and neuroticism. These dimensions provide a comprehensive and systematic way to evaluate individual differences in behavior, emotions, and thought processes.

Openness refers to an individual's willingness to embrace new experiences, ideas, and perspectives. People who score high in openness are often curious, imaginative, and creative. They tend to seek novelty and enjoy exploring abstract concepts. In contrast, individuals with low openness are more practical, conventional, and resistant to change, often preferring familiar routines.

Conscientiousness describes an individual's level of organization, discipline, and reliability. Highly conscientious people are responsible, goal-oriented, and detail-focused. They excel in planning and maintaining structure in their personal and professional lives. On the other hand, individuals with low conscientiousness may be more spontaneous, careless, or inconsistent in their actions.

Extraversion measures the extent to which an individual is outgoing and energized by social interactions. Highly extraverted individuals are sociable, assertive, and enthusiastic, often thriving in group settings. Those with low extraversion, or introverts, prefer solitude, tend to be more reserved, and may find social situations draining.

Agreeableness reflects an individual's tendency to be cooperative, compassionate, and harmonious in interactions with others. Highly agreeable individuals are empathetic, considerate, and eager to avoid conflict. In contrast, those with low agreeableness may be more competitive, skeptical, or confrontational, prioritizing their own needs over others'.

Neuroticism refers to an individual's emotional stability and ability to handle stress. People high in neuroticism are more prone to experiencing negative emotions such as anxiety, depression, and irritability. They may struggle to cope with challenges effectively. Conversely, individuals with low neuroticism tend to be calm, resilient, and emotionally stable, even in difficult situations.

The Five-Factor Model is considered universal, as it has been validated across cultures and populations. Research has shown that these dimensions are relatively stable over time and are influenced by both genetic and environmental factors. This universality makes the model a valuable tool for understanding personality across different contexts.

The model has practical applications in various fields, including education, organizational psychology, and mental health. For instance, conscientious individuals often perform well in structured work environments, while extraverts may excel in roles requiring teamwork and leadership. Similarly, understanding an individual's agreeableness can be critical in conflict resolution and relationship building.

In addition to its practical use, the Five-Factor Model has contributed to academic research by providing a framework for studying personality's impact on behavior, cognition, and emotions. It has also advanced understanding of how personality traits influence life outcomes, such as career success, relationships, and mental health.

While the Five-Factor Model captures a broad spectrum of personality traits, it is not without limitations. Critics argue that it does not fully account for specific aspects of personality, such as morality, spirituality, or situational variability. Despite these critiques, the model remains a cornerstone in personality psychology due to its simplicity and empirical support.

In conclusion, the Five-Factor Model offers a robust framework for understanding personality, emphasizing five key dimensions that shape human behavior and interactions. By providing insights into individual differences, it serves as both a theoretical foundation and a practical tool for personal and professional development. This model continues to be a vital resource in the study of personality and its influence on human life.

2.2.2. The Relationship Between Consciousness and the Subconscious

The relationship between consciousness and the subconscious is one of the most intriguing topics in psychology, as it explores how these two aspects of the mind interact and influence human behavior. Consciousness refers to the state of awareness, where thoughts, feelings, and perceptions are actively processed. In contrast, the subconscious operates below the level of conscious awareness, storing information and experiences that subtly influence thoughts, emotions, and actions.

Sigmund Freud, a pioneer in psychoanalytic theory, described the mind as an iceberg. The visible tip represents consciousness, while the vast submerged portion symbolizes the subconscious and unconscious mind. According to Freud, the subconscious acts as a repository for thoughts, memories, and desires that are not immediately accessible but still shape conscious behavior

The subconscious mind plays a critical role in decision-making and problem-solving. Many decisions that appear rational on the surface are often influenced by subconscious experiences, biases, and emotions. For instance, an individual's instinctive reaction to a situation might be shaped by memories or patterns stored in the subconscious.

Dreams are another way the subconscious communicates with consciousness. Freud believed that dreams are a gateway to the subconscious, allowing suppressed thoughts and desires to surface in symbolic forms. Modern psychology continues to study dreams as a means of understanding subconscious processes.

Habits and automatic behaviors are also deeply tied to the subconscious. Actions performed without conscious effort, such as driving a familiar route or tying shoelaces, are managed by the subconscious mind. These routines allow the conscious mind to focus on more complex tasks while the subconscious handles repetitive actions.

The relationship between consciousness and the subconscious is bidirectional. While the subconscious influences conscious thoughts and behaviors, conscious actions and decisions can also reshape the subconscious. For example, repeated affirmations or mindfulness practices can alter subconscious beliefs, leading to changes in behavior and emotional well-being.

The subconscious is not static; it is constantly processing and organizing information from experiences, emotions, and sensory inputs. Even when the conscious mind is at rest, such as during sleep, the subconscious continues to work, consolidating memories and integrating new knowledge.

Emotional responses often originate in the subconscious. For example, a person might feel anxiety in a particular situation without understanding why. This response may stem from a past experience stored in the subconscious that the conscious mind has forgotten or suppressed.

The subconscious can also act as a protective mechanism. Traumatic experiences, for instance, are sometimes repressed into the subconscious to shield the individual from immediate emotional distress. While this may provide temporary relief, unresolved subconscious conflicts can resurface in the form of psychological or physical symptoms.

Techniques such as hypnosis, meditation, and psychotherapy aim to bridge the gap between consciousness and the subconscious. By bringing subconscious thoughts and memories to the surface, individuals can gain insight into their emotions and behaviors, allowing for healing and personal growth.

The relationship between consciousness and the subconscious is essential for understanding human creativity. Subconscious processes often generate ideas and solutions that surface during conscious moments, such as the sudden "aha" moments of insight or inspiration.

In conclusion, the interplay between consciousness and the subconscious is a dynamic and continuous process. The subconscious serves as a vast reservoir of experiences and emotions that influence conscious thoughts and actions, while the conscious mind has the power to shape and modify subconscious patterns.

Understanding this relationship provides valuable insights into human behavior, emotional well-being, and personal development.

2.2.3. The Structure of Consciousness in Modern Neuroscience

Modern neuroscience focuses on understanding the structure of consciousness through biological and cognitive processes. Consciousness is defined as the complex mechanism that enables individuals to be aware of themselves and their surroundings. Neuroscience seeks to explain this mechanism through the dynamic interactions and neural networks across different regions of the brain.

One of the foundational components of consciousness is the **prefrontal cortex,** which serves as the center for higher-order cognitive functions such as reasoning, planning, and decision-making. This region allows individuals to focus attention, evaluate alternatives, and make conscious choices, functioning as the executive center of consciousness.

The **parietal cortex** is another critical area involved in consciousness. It is responsible for processing sensory information and maintaining spatial awareness. The parietal cortex helps individuals comprehend their environment and position themselves physically within it.

Research in neuroscience has demonstrated that consciousness is not localized to a single brain region but instead requires information sharing and integration among various brain areas. The **Global Workspace Theory** suggests that consciousness emerges from synchronized neural activity across multiple regions of the brain. According to this theory, consciousness acts as a global information network encompassing different brain areas.

Consciousness arises from the interaction of neurons in the brain through electrical and chemical signals. Techniques such as **functional magnetic resonance imaging (fMRI)** and **electroencephalography (EEG)** are used to observe which brain regions are active during conscious experiences. These tools provide deeper insights into the neural basis of consciousness.

Deep brain structures like the **thalamus** also play a significant role in the structure of consciousness. The thalamus acts as a relay station, transmitting sensory information to the cortex and contributing to the maintenance of conscious awareness. Damage to the thalamus can lead to severe disruptions in consciousness.

Levels of consciousness range from states of full wakefulness to deep sleep. The brain's reticular activating system regulates these levels, playing a critical role in maintaining wakefulness, sustaining attention, and responding to environmental stimuli.

In neuroscience, consciousness is not limited to awareness; it also includes subjective experiences. This distinction is often categorized into **phenomenal consciousness and access consciousness.** Phenomenal consciousness deals with how individuals experience the world, while access consciousness involves the ability to recall and use those experiences consciously.

Neuroscientists emphasize the importance of **neural correlates of consciousness (NCC)** in understanding its structure. This approach identifies specific patterns of brain activity associated with particular conscious states. For example, the conscious perception of a visual experience is linked to distinct activity patterns in the visual cortex.

Consciousness has been shown to have a dynamic structure that continuously shifts between different states. Conscious experiences balance past memories, present conditions, and future expectations, reflecting the brain's constant processing and updating of information.

Modern neuroscience highlights that consciousness is not only a biological mechanism but also shaped by social and environmental contexts. The way the brain processes sensory information from the external world and assigns meaning to it forms the foundation of conscious experiences.

Consciousness is also flexible, thanks to the brain's neuroplasticity. Processes such as learning, habit formation, and acquiring new skills demonstrate the adaptable nature of consciousness. This flexibility allows individuals to redefine their interactions with themselves and their surroundings.

In conclusion, modern neuroscience has made significant advances in understanding the structure of consciousness. However, due to its complexity and multidimensional nature, many questions remain unanswered. Understanding consciousness is not only a scientific pursuit but also essential for individuals to gain deeper insight into themselves and their interactions with the world. This understanding contributes to both personal awareness and enhanced social connections.

2.3. HUMAN MEMORY AND THE DIGITIZATION OF MEMORIES

Human memory is a complex system that enables individuals to store past experiences, knowledge, and emotional states. With the rapid advancement of modern technology, the idea of digitizing this uniquely human capability has become a central topic of scientific and ethical discussions. The digitization of memory holds the potential to record, preserve, and make human experiences accessible in the future.

Human memory operates through three fundamental processes: encoding, storage, and retrieval. Encoding transforms sensory inputs into memories, storage keeps these memories in short- or long-term repositories, and retrieval allows individuals to access this information when needed. The digitization of memory seeks to replicate some or all of these processes in digital systems.

Digitizing memories requires understanding the structure of biological memory and modeling it in digital systems. Neural networks in the human brain offer a source of inspiration for this endeavor. Neuroscientific research has revealed the critical role of the hippocampus in forming and storing memories, providing insights into how memories might be digitized.

The digitization process involves capturing, organizing, and reconstructing human memory using digital devices or artificial intelligence systems. For example, brain-computer interfaces (BCIs) have the potential to transfer thoughts and memories directly into a digital platform, extending the boundaries of biological memory.

Digitizing memories has transformative potential at both individual and societal levels. Individuals could preserve important memories they do not want to forget, enabling them to access these memories in the future. Additionally, this technology could help recover lost information or emotional experiences.

Digitized memories could revolutionize education and learning processes. Instead of relying solely on memorization, students could access digital memory platforms to enhance their learning experiences. Moreover, digital memory could increase intellectual capacity by providing constant access to knowledge.

However, the digitization of memories raises significant ethical and social questions. Who owns a digitized memory? How should a person's digital memories be preserved or utilized after their death? These questions are critical ethical concerns that must be addressed in developing digital memory technologies.

Security is one of the most significant challenges in digital memory. Digitized memories could be manipulated or stolen by malicious actors. Therefore, ensuring the secure storage and restricted access to these data is of paramount importance.

The accuracy of digitized memories is another area of concern. Human memory is often biased and malleable; individuals reinterpret or modify their memories over time. How will digital systems manage this variability, and how can they determine whether a memory truly represents an authentic experience?

The societal implications of this technology are also noteworthy. People could continuously revisit past events through digitized memories, potentially limiting their ability to focus on the future. Constant accessibility to memories might lead individuals to become emotionally trapped in the past.

Digital memory technologies could also reshape concepts of identity and individuality. If all of a person's memories are stored on a digital platform, at what point is their "self" defined? How will digitized memories influence personal and social identities?

The medical applications of this technology are vast. For instance, digitized memories could help individuals with neurological conditions like Alzheimer's recover lost memories. Additionally, the technology could be used for therapeutic purposes, helping individuals reinterpret and process traumatic memories.

The digitization of memories is not merely a technological innovation but an existential transformation for humanity. Transferring human memory to digital platforms could expand the boundaries of human nature and existence. However, it is crucial to develop this technology ethically and with a focus on human well-being.

In conclusion, the digitization of human memory has the potential to be a revolutionary scientific and technological breakthrough. While offering immense opportunities, it also brings ethical, social, and security challenges that must be addressed. The digitization of memory stands as a development that could redefine human nature and life experiences in the future.

2.3.1. The Suitability of Brain Structures for Digital Modeling

The human brain is a complex structure that functions as the biological center for thought, emotion, and behavior. Advances in technology have accelerated efforts to digitally model this intricate system. The suitability of brain structures for digital modeling depends on understanding biological processes and replicating them in artificial systems.

One of the most suitable structures for digital modeling is neurons. The human brain contains approximately 86 billion neurons, which communicate and process information through synapses. Artificial neural networks, inspired by these biological processes, simulate neurons in digital form. These models are used to replicate brain functions in artificial intelligence systems.

Synapses, the connections between neurons, regulate the flow of information. Synaptic connections are the foundation of learning and memory processes. Digital modeling aims to simulate these synaptic interactions to mimic learning mechanisms. Deep learning algorithms are designed based on the principles of synaptic activity.

The brain's electrical activity is another feature well-suited for digital modeling. Communication between neurons occurs through electrical signals, which can be measured using technologies such as electroencephalography (EEG). These measurements provide foundational data for simulating brain activities in digital systems.

The hippocampus, which plays a critical role in memory and learning, is a key focus for digital modeling. This region is vital for transferring information from short-term to long-term memory. The modeling of the hippocampus is particularly useful for developing artificial memory systems, as artificial intelligence applications seek to emulate its processes.

The prefrontal cortex, responsible for decision-making, planning, and problem-solving, is another critical region for modeling. Digital models of the prefrontal cortex enable artificial intelligence systems to simulate complex decision-making processes. Algorithms inspired by the prefrontal cortex enhance the capabilities of robotic systems, making them smarter and more efficient.

The thalamus, which serves as a relay station for sensory information to the cortex, plays a crucial role in maintaining conscious awareness. In digital modeling, the thalamus's role in filtering and directing information can be applied to data processing systems, particularly in analyzing sensory inputs.

The motor cortex, which controls movement, has also been successfully modeled in robotics. Robotic technologies replicate the functioning of the motor cortex to develop systems that mimic human movements. For example, prosthetic limbs and humanoid robots are designed using algorithms based on motor cortex functions.

The limbic system, which is essential for processing emotions, is another focus of digital modeling. The amygdala, a component of the limbic system, regulates basic emotions such as fear and anger. Digital modeling of these regions aims to give artificial intelligence systems emotional intelligence and the ability to process emotional responses.

Digital modeling of the brain also incorporates the principle of neuroplasticity. The brain's ability to learn and restructure itself inspires the development of flexible algorithms in digital systems. Learning machines, for instance, are designed to evolve continuously, mimicking the brain's plasticity.

One of the biggest challenges in modeling brain structures is the inability to fully replicate biological complexity. The brain is not just a network of neurons; it is a dynamic system shaped by chemical signals, genetic factors, and environmental interactions. Digital modeling simplifies this multidimensional structure while striving to maintain its functional integrity.

Ethical considerations also play a significant role in brain modeling. Digitally replicating brain structures may affect individual identity and privacy. For instance, transferring a person's thoughts into a digital model raises concerns about privacy rights and data security.

In conclusion, the suitability of human brain structures for digital modeling depends on a deep understanding of biological processes. Neurons, synapses, electrical activity, and various brain regions provide critical inspiration for the development of artificial systems. However, this process faces both technological limitations and ethical challenges. Brain modeling holds immense potential not only as a tool for understanding human nature but also as a way to push the boundaries of technological innovation.

2.3.2. The Transferability of Memories and Emotions to Artificial Intelligence

The transfer of memories and emotions to artificial intelligence (AI) is based on the idea of replicating and simulating human experiences in digital platforms. This field lies at the intersection of neuroscience, AI, psychology, and ethics. Transferring these two fundamental elements of the human mind to artificial systems holds significant technological and philosophical potential.

Memories are formed through processes of encoding, storage, and retrieval within the brain's neural networks. The transferability of memories to AI relies on simulating these connections in digital environments. Brain-computer interfaces (BCIs) are an essential technology that allows individuals to directly transfer thoughts and memories to a digital platform.

The primary challenge of transferring memories lies in the complexity of human memory. Memory is not merely the storage of information but also the emotional and contextual elements that give it meaning. AI relies on deep learning algorithms and big data analytics to understand and replicate this complexity.

The transfer of emotions to AI presents a different set of challenges. Emotions are not solely the product of chemical and electrical activity in the brain; they are also influenced by past experiences, genetic predispositions, and environmental factors. Efforts to develop emotional intelligence (EQ) in AI aim to imbue artificial systems with human-like emotional responses.

One key tool in transferring emotions to AI is emotion analysis, which interprets emotional states through cues such as facial expressions, tone of voice, and body language. This enables AI systems to interact with individuals in a more natural and emotionally intelligent manner. However, digitally simulating emotions does not equate to creating genuine emotional experiences.

The transfer of memories to AI also involves digitizing memory systems. For example, individuals' memories of specific events could be stored on a digital platform and retrieved when needed. This capability allows AI to understand an individual's past and make decisions aligned with that context.

Transferring memories and emotions to AI essentially involves digitally replicating a part of human identity. This process has the potential to create a digital reflection or "digital twin" of an individual. However, the extent to which such a reflection accurately represents a person's true identity remains a contentious issue.

Ethical concerns pose significant barriers to implementing this technology. Digitally transferring memories and emotions raises questions about privacy, consent, and data security. For instance, the misuse or manipulation of an individual's memories could have profound consequences, underscoring the need for an ethical framework.

Another challenge is the subjective nature of human memories and emotions. Memories are often shaped by an individual's perspective and can change over time. AI faces limitations in managing this variability and determining the "authentic" version of a memory.

The transfer of memories and emotions to AI holds significant potential in medical applications. For example, in treating conditions like Alzheimer's or post-traumatic stress disorder (PTSD), digitally reconstructing memories and emotional responses could aid in therapeutic processes.

The integration of memories and emotions into AI could also transform human-machine interactions. Systems that respond with more human-like emotions could enable individuals to form stronger emotional connections with technology, especially in fields like social robotics and virtual assistants.

The transfer of memories and emotions can also contribute to creative processes. AI could use individuals' past experiences and emotional states as inspiration to create artistic or literary works, pushing the boundaries of human-machine collaboration.

Technological limitations are a critical factor affecting the success of this process. The inability to fully simulate the biological processes of the human brain poses challenges in ensuring the accuracy of memories and emotions transferred to AI. This raises critical questions about how such technology will evolve in the future.

In conclusion, the transferability of memories and emotions to AI offers significant opportunities and challenges for humanity. This process is not just a technological innovation but also raises profound philosophical questions about human nature and identity.

The replication of memories and emotions in digital systems has the potential to blur the lines between humans and machines.

However, this technology requires careful consideration of its scientific, ethical, social, and psychological dimensions.

These developments open new horizons for how human experiences can integrate with AI and how this integration will shape human life. Memories and emotions not only help AI become more human-like but also enable technology to serve humanity in a meaningful way.

2.4. HUMANOID ROBOTS AND HUMANITY: A NEW PERSPECTIVE

Humanoid robots represent a groundbreaking innovation that reflects humanity in its most technologically advanced form. These robots aim to replicate human features, movements, and behaviors, providing not only a technical achievement but also a new perspective on the nature of being human and societal roles.

The development of humanoid robots requires a deep understanding of human anatomy and behavior. Their facial expressions, body movements, and tone of voice enable them to interact with humans more naturally. This advancement elevates human-robot interactions to a more empathetic and meaningful level, creating new applications in various social contexts.

One of the most striking aspects of humanoid robots is their potential to serve as both helpers and complements to humanity. For instance, they can be employed in elderly care, education, or hazardous environments, alleviating physical and mental burdens. Such applications highlight their contribution to enhancing human quality of life.

However, humanoid robots raise profound questions about humanity and ethical values beyond their functional innovation.

When a robot resembles a human so closely, how do people form relationships with these machines? Can uniquely human emotions like empathy, love, or respect be genuinely experienced with a humanoid robot? These questions compel us to rethink the boundaries of human nature.

The presence of humanoid robots may also impact human identity and societal roles. Their ability to fully replace humans in certain tasks could redefine humanity's role in the workforce and reshape perceptions of productivity. Additionally, the human-like features of robots may lead individuals to question their own humanity and self-identity.

Ethical considerations are central to the development of humanoid robots. When robots are treated as humans, will they have rights or responsibilities? More importantly, what risks does such technology pose if misused? Issues such as the influence of robots on human decision-making processes and individual freedoms must be carefully addressed.

From a technological standpoint, the development of humanoid robots has driven significant advancements in artificial intelligence and robotics engineering. Robots equipped with emotional intelligence are particularly noteworthy for their ability to form emotional bonds with humans. These technological achievements allow robots to transcend their mechanical nature and be perceived as social entities.

The societal acceptance of humanoid robots depends not only on their functionality but also on cultural and psychological factors. Different societies may perceive humanoid robots differently. In some cultures, robots are seen as friendly helpers, while in others, they might be viewed as threats. Therefore, the design and applications of humanoid robots must consider cultural sensitivities.

In conclusion, humanoid robots represent a technological milestone that offers humanity new opportunities and responsibilities. These robots are not merely tools but also mirrors prompting humanity to reassess its nature and societal structure. The development of humanoid robots blurs the boundaries between humanity and technology in unprecedented ways, building a future that is both promising and complex.

2.4.1. Physical Features of Humanoid Robots and Human Interaction

Humanoid robots are machines designed to mimic human physical features and behaviors. Their physical structures are developed to closely resemble human anatomy, aiming to create natural and meaningful interactions with humans. This resemblance facilitates their integration into human environments and enhances their functionality in various applications.

The most prominent physical feature of humanoid robots is their human-like anatomy, including two arms, two legs, and a head. This structure enables them to perform tasks in environments designed for humans, such as using tools or navigating spaces like homes or offices. Their design allows them to adapt to everyday human surroundings seamlessly.

The facial design of humanoid robots plays a crucial role in effective communication. Facial expressions, eye contact, and micro-expressions are integrated into their design to enhance emotional interactions. The ability to understand and respond to human facial cues helps robots appear more empathetic and relatable.

The physical movements of humanoid robots are developed to replicate human-like motion. Mechanisms that mimic joints and muscles allow them to walk, sit, and grasp objects naturally. This not only improves their functionality but also makes their interactions more acceptable and comfortable for humans.

Voice communication is another critical aspect of humanoid robots' interaction capabilities. Using natural language processing and voice recognition technologies, these robots can converse fluently with humans. Adjusting speech tone and pace to resemble human conversation further enhances the effectiveness of their communication.

Tactile feedback systems in humanoid robots also strengthen human-robot interaction. Skin-like surfaces equipped with sensors create a sense of touch, enabling robots to respond to physical contact. This feature increases safety and supports emotional bonding between humans and robots.

In designing humanoid robots, balancing aesthetics and functionality is essential. An overly mechanical or cold appearance can hinder emotional connections with humans. As a result, their design is optimized to be both visually appealing and functionally effective.

The physical features of humanoid robots are also critical for safety. Since they interact closely with humans, their design must minimize the risk of accidents. Flexible motion mechanisms and sensor-equipped systems enhance safety and allow the robots to perform tasks with precision.

Humanoid robots' physical features are not limited to individual interactions but also play a vital role in social contexts. For instance, their design enables them to move seamlessly in crowded environments, making them particularly effective in healthcare, education, and public service applications.

Physical resemblance is a key factor in building empathy and trust between humans and humanoid robots. People are more likely to form emotional connections with robots that share human-like features. This connection makes robots more effective in roles such as social robotics, therapy, and customer service.

The physical design of humanoid robots not only replicates human interactions but also makes these interactions more efficient and effective. Robots can observe human behavior during tasks and adapt accordingly, enhancing their learning and adaptability.

Cultural factors can also influence the physical design of humanoid robots. Different cultures may have varying preferences for the appearance and behavior of robots. While some cultures may favor robots that closely resemble humans, others might prefer a more mechanical aesthetic.

The physical features of humanoid robots enable them to collaborate effectively with humans. Whether in industrial settings or everyday life, ergonomic and compatible designs allow robots to work alongside humans efficiently, enhancing productivity and cooperation.

In conclusion, the physical features of humanoid robots play a crucial role in enabling effective and natural interactions with humans. Human-like design not only enhances their functionality but also fosters emotional connections. These robots represent a technical and social revolution with the potential to become an integral part of human life in the future.

2.4.2. Redefining the Physical and Digital Boundaries of Being Human

Humanity is undergoing a transformative period where the lines between physical and digital boundaries are increasingly blurred due to rapid technological advancements. The concept of being human is expanding beyond biological existence, finding a new place in the digital realm. This shift necessitates a redefinition of human nature on both individual and societal levels.

Physical boundaries have traditionally been defined by the limitations and capabilities of the human body. However, innovations such as biotechnology and artificial organs are extending these boundaries. Prosthetic limbs, neural-connected devices, and other bio-integration technologies are transforming the human body into not just a biological entity but also a technological one.

Digital boundaries, on the other hand, concern the existence of individuals in the digital world. Social media, virtual reality, and digital identities allow individuals to exist in a new dimension online. Digital identities enable the creation of a "cyber self" parallel to one's physical existence, demonstrating the multi-layered nature of humanity.

Artificial intelligence (AI) and robotics further expand the boundaries of being human. AI systems and humanoid robots capable of exhibiting human-like thought and behavior challenge the distinctions between human and machine. This development raises philosophical and ethical questions about the essence of being human.

The digitization of memories and emotions represents another intersection of physical and digital boundaries. When human memories can be transferred to AI systems and processed digitally, the human experience gains a digital dimension. This creates a new concept of immortality for humanity.

The idea of digital immortality is based on the possibility of transferring human consciousness to digital platforms, allowing individuals to exist beyond the limitations of their physical bodies. This demonstrates that the boundaries of being human are no longer confined to physical existence but are redefined by digital continuity.

The redefinition of physical and digital boundaries has profound implications for human identity. The integration of technology into daily life is reshaping how individuals define themselves. A person's identity is now shaped not only by their biological characteristics but also by their presence in the digital world.

This transformation also raises ethical and social questions. The digitization of humanity introduces challenges related to privacy, data security, and individual freedoms. For example, the manipulation or misuse of an individual's digital identity necessitates the establishment of a new framework for human rights.

On a societal level, the redefinition of physical and digital boundaries creates new social dynamics. Digital technologies are transforming the ways individuals interact with each other and laying the foundation for a global digital society. This, in turn, necessitates the redefinition of social bonds and relationships.

The merging of digital and physical boundaries is revolutionizing fields such as education, healthcare, and the workforce. In education, virtual reality and AI-based systems personalize learning experiences. In healthcare, digitized biological data enhances patient care and treatment processes.

The redefinition of physical and digital boundaries is not merely technological progress but also an evolution of human nature. As humanity extends its physical boundaries, it simultaneously gains new meaning as a digital entity. This process bridges biological and digital elements, fostering both individual and collective rebirth.

In conclusion, the redefinition of physical and digital boundaries is a transformative process that fundamentally alters the meaning and potential of being human. While this shift offers new opportunities, it also brings forth ethical, social, and philosophical questions. The transition beyond the physical and digital boundaries of being human stands as one of the most significant changes shaping the future of the world.

3. COPYING HUMAN PERSONALITY WITH ARTIFICIAL INTELLIGENCE

Copying human personality with artificial intelligence (AI) refers to the complex and ambitious process of replicating an individual's thoughts, behaviors, and emotional structure in a digital system. This idea represents one of the most advanced goals of AI technologies, aiming to recreate the essence of a person in a digital environment. However, this technological endeavor raises numerous scientific and ethical questions.

Human personality is the sum of an individual's emotions, thoughts, and behaviors, shaped by complex interactions of neurological, psychological, and social factors. Replicating this structure involves understanding the workings of the human brain and integrating them into an AI system. This process requires accurately modeling the fundamental building blocks of personality.

The first step in digitizing personality is understanding an individual's behavioral and emotional patterns. AI can analyze a person's past decisions, reactions, and preferences using big data analytics and machine learning algorithms. These data can then be used to create a digital profile that reflects the individual's personality traits.

Another approach to copying personality involves neuroscience and brain-computer interfaces (BCIs). By digitally monitoring and recording neural activity in the brain, thoughts and emotions can potentially be transferred to an AI system. This method provides a foundation for developing algorithms that mimic the brain's electrical and chemical processes.

One of the biggest challenges in copying personality is the dynamic and ever-changing nature of human personality. People evolve constantly based on their experiences, learning, and environmental conditions. For AI to accurately replicate this, it must capture this variability and model the individual's transformation over time.

Emotional intelligence is a critical component of human personality that must also be integrated into AI systems. AI can analyze facial expressions, vocal tones, and behavioral patterns to understand an individual's emotional state. However, how these emotional states are represented and processed in a digital environment remains an ongoing challenge.

The ethical dimension is one of the most debated aspects of copying human personality with AI. The implications for privacy, freedom, and identity rights are significant. For instance, when a personality is copied, who controls this digital copy, and how is it used? These are critical ethical concerns that must be addressed

The process also raises questions of authenticity and identity. Can a digital copy truly be a faithful representation of an individual? If an AI system can perfectly replicate a person's thoughts and behaviors, should it be considered the same as the person themselves? These questions lead to deeper philosophical discussions about the essence of being human.

From a technological perspective, copying human personality offers significant opportunities to enhance AI's learning capabilities. Deep learning algorithms and neural networks are particularly effective tools for analyzing and reproducing thought processes and behavioral patterns. These technologies form the backbone of personality replication.

Copying human personality pushes the boundaries of psychology and neuroscience. Understanding the brain's chemical, electrical, and biological mechanisms is key to recreating these processes in a digital system. However, this endeavor is still incomplete and faces significant technical limitations.

AI's ability to replicate personality has tremendous potential in medical applications. For example, in conditions like Alzheimer's, digitally preserving a person's personality and memories could improve patients' quality of life. Additionally, this technology could be used for therapeutic purposes, helping individuals process and reinterpret traumatic experiences.

Another potential application of personality replication is in education and the workplace. AI could adapt to individuals' learning styles and work habits, creating more effective models for education and collaboration. This personalized experience could enhance productivity and engagement.

However, the societal implications of this technology must also be considered. Digitally replicating human personality could have profound effects on social relationships, labor markets, and cultural values. The blurring boundaries between humans and AI raise new ethical and social questions in a broader context.

The future applications of copying human personality with AI could redefine the relationship between humans and machines. Systems capable of digitally representing human behaviors and thoughts could create new opportunities for humanity while also introducing new challenges and risks.

In conclusion, copying human personality with AI is a process that pushes the boundaries of technology and raises fundamental questions about human nature. This endeavor is not just a technical achievement but also represents a philosophical and ethical transformation for humanity.

Transferring human personality into AI systems is a technological milestone with profound implications not only for individuals but also for societies. This development redefines the meaning of being human and lays the foundation for future human-machine relationships.

3.1. WHAT IS ARTIFICIAL INTELLIGENCE AND HOW DOES IT WORK?

Artificial intelligence (AI) refers to computer systems and algorithms designed to mimic human-like thinking, learning, and problem-solving abilities. This technology, modeled on human intelligence, enables machines to perceive environmental data, interpret it, make logical decisions, and improve themselves over time. AI is a groundbreaking innovation transforming various sectors, including healthcare, education, industry, and finance.

AI typically operates through subfields such as machine learning, deep learning, and natural language processing. Machine learning enables systems to learn from large datasets and make predictions without being explicitly programmed. Deep learning, inspired by neural networks, allows for more complex learning processes by recognizing patterns in vast amounts of data.

A fundamental component of AI is algorithms. Algorithms are mathematical and statistical formulas used to analyze data, build models, and generate outcomes. These algorithms determine the learning and problem-solving capacity of AI systems. For instance, in a recommendation system, algorithms analyze user preferences to provide personalized suggestions

AI systems rely heavily on large volumes of data. This data serves as the foundation for AI to learn and make decisions. For example, a facial recognition system analyzes thousands of images to develop the ability to recognize facial features. This process enables AI to perform specific tasks more efficiently.

Natural language processing (NLP) is a subfield of AI that enables systems to interact with human language. NLP analyzes text and speech to derive meaning and facilitates more natural communication with humans. For example, a voice assistant understands user commands, provides responses, and performs specific tasks.

AI systems continuously improve themselves through feedback mechanisms. These systems evaluate new information from users or the environment to optimize their performance. This feature is critical for applications such as autonomous vehicles or recommendation systems, which require constant adaptation and improvement.

The success of AI is closely tied to advancements in computing power and big data technologies. Modern AI systems can process vast amounts of data quickly and efficiently, a feat that was impossible in the past. This increased capacity allows AI to solve more complex problems and be applied across a broader range of domains.

While AI offers many benefits that simplify human life, it also raises ethical and security concerns. Issues such as biases in AI systems, data security, and the impact on the workforce highlight the need for responsible AI development. Additionally, the uncontrolled use of AI poses risks to both individuals and societies.

In conclusion, artificial intelligence is a powerful technology that mimics human intelligence and provides solutions in various fields. Built on algorithms, big data, and learning processes, AI is rapidly expanding and shaping the technological infrastructure of the future. However, addressing its potential risks and ethical responsibilities is crucial to ensuring the sustainable and safe development of AI.

3.1.1. Machine Learning, Deep Learning, and Data Processing Techniques

Machine learning is a branch of artificial intelligence that enables computers to learn without being explicitly programmed. It involves analyzing data to identify patterns and make predictions. Machine learning is a powerful tool for solving complex problems by extracting insights from large datasets. Today, it has wide applications across industries such as finance, healthcare, and e-commerce.

At the core of machine learning are methods like supervised learning, unsupervised learning, and reinforcement learning. Supervised learning relies on labeled datasets to make accurate predictions. For example, an email filtering system distinguishes between spam and legitimate emails based on labeled data. Unsupervised learning, on the other hand, identifies patterns and groups within unlabeled data. Reinforcement learning uses reward and penalty mechanisms to improve decision-making capabilities.

Deep learning, a subset of machine learning, employs artificial neural networks inspired by biological neurons. Deep learning algorithms process large amounts of data through multi-layered neural networks, enabling more complex and abstract information extraction. This approach has achieved groundbreaking success in areas like image recognition, natural language processing, and autonomous vehicles.

The success of deep learning is largely attributed to access to large datasets and advanced computational power. In image recognition systems, deep learning algorithms analyze millions of images to achieve high accuracy in tasks like facial recognition or object classification. This method enhances the ability to learn from data and enables the development of systems capable of human-level decision-making.

Data processing techniques form the foundation of machine learning and deep learning workflows. Raw data must be cleaned, transformed, and optimized before analysis. Preprocessing steps include handling missing values, removing outliers, and normalizing data. These steps are critical for improving the performance of learning algorithms.

Big data technologies further enhance the efficiency of machine learning and deep learning. Platforms like Hadoop and Spark enable the processing of large-scale datasets. These tools allow data to be processed in a distributed manner, facilitating the rapid training of complex models.

Model evaluation and optimization techniques are also crucial in machine learning and deep learning applications. Methods like cross-validation, error analysis, and accuracy metrics are used to measure model reliability and effectiveness. Additionally, hyperparameter optimization can further enhance model performance.

In conclusion, machine learning, deep learning, and data processing techniques are powerful tools that form the backbone of modern technology. Combined with big data and advanced computational power, these methods are employed to solve complex problems and develop smarter systems. Technical expertise and ethical considerations are essential to ensure the responsible and effective application of these technologies.

3.1.2. Modeling Human Language with Natural Language Processing (NLP)

Natural Language Processing (NLP) is a discipline that combines artificial intelligence and computer science to understand, process, and generate human language. By processing inputs like text and speech, NLP enables machines to communicate with humans in a natural way. This technology powers applications ranging from translation systems to chatbots and makes it possible to model human language in digital systems.

Human language comprises multiple layers, including grammar, semantics, context, and emotional tone. NLP develops algorithms to analyze these elements for a deeper understanding of language. For example, syntactic analysis examines word phrases and sentence structures to ensure that language is processed according to grammatical rules.

A crucial aspect of NLP is semantic analysis, which focuses on understanding the meaning of words and sentences within context. The same word can carry different meanings depending on the context. NLP models are trained on large datasets to resolve contextual meanings. For instance, the meaning of a word is determined by its relationship to other words in the sentence.

Language modeling is a cornerstone of NLP and involves creating a mathematical representation of language to digitally replicate it. Modern language models, especially those based on deep learning, learn the structure and patterns of language. Transformer-based models, such as GPT, can generate human-like text and effectively model the complexities of language.

Sentiment analysis is another important NLP technique for modeling human language. This technique identifies the emotional tone expressed in text or speech. For example, NLP tools can analyze customer feedback to classify sentiments as positive, negative, or neutral.

The success of NLP is directly tied to large language datasets and robust computational infrastructure. Extensive text datasets are used to train language models, teaching them the natural flow and complexity of language. This enables NLP systems to make more precise and accurate predictions.

Translation systems are one of the most common applications of NLP. NLP algorithms consider grammatical rules, cultural context, and linguistic nuances when translating text from one language to another. Models used in machine translation are continuously updated and refined, producing increasingly high-quality results.

Voice assistants and chatbots are other examples of NLP's ability to model human language. These systems understand users' natural language requests and provide appropriate responses.

Techniques such as Natural Language Understanding (NLU) and Natural Language Generation (NLG) play a critical role in such applications.

In conclusion, Natural Language Processing (NLP) enables machines to use language in a human-like way by modeling the complexities of grammar, context, emotion, and meaning. By processing these layers, NLP provides a powerful technology for both individual users and industries. With advancing models and data processing techniques, NLP continues to revolutionize human-machine communication.

3.2. COLLECTION AND ANALYSIS OF HUMAN DATA

The collection and analysis of human data have become fundamental components of modern technology. The vast amount of data generated by individuals through digital devices, social media, healthcare applications, and other platforms provides valuable insights at both individual and societal levels. While this process enables a deeper understanding of behaviors, preferences, and needs, it also raises ethical and privacy concerns.

The data collection process is typically carried out through two primary methods: active and passive data collection. Active data collection requires individuals to provide information directly, such as filling out surveys or sharing details on an application. Passive data collection, on the other hand, involves gathering data without the individual's explicit awareness, such as internet browsing history, app usage, or location tracking.

Collected human data can be categorized into various types. Demographic data (age, gender, education level), behavioral data (shopping habits, online activities), and biometric data (heart rate, facial recognition data) are among the key categories. When aggregated, this data can be used to create personal profiles and better understand user needs.

Data analysis is the process of making collected information meaningful. Big data analytics employs various techniques to identify patterns, trends, and relationships within complex datasets. Machine learning algorithms are a cornerstone of this process, enabling automated processing and interpretation of data.

The analysis of human data has led to groundbreaking applications across numerous industries. In healthcare, data is used to monitor patient health and enable early diagnosis of diseases. In education, data analytics serves as a tool for tracking student performance and personalizing learning experiences.

In marketing and advertising, human data analysis helps businesses better understand target audiences and create personalized campaigns. E-commerce platforms analyze users' shopping histories to provide tailored recommendations and boost sales. However, this also raises concerns about individuals' privacy.

Data security is a critical concern in the collection and analysis of human data. Misuse of collected data, identity theft, or unauthorized sharing can have serious consequences. Strong encryption methods and legal regulations are essential to ensure data is stored and processed securely.

Ethical issues are a significant area of discussion in human data collection and analysis. Collecting data without individuals' consent can violate their privacy. Transparency in data collection processes and obtaining informed consent from individuals are crucial for the responsible application of these technologies.

The processes of data collection and analysis are creating a significant transformation in how technology impacts human lives.

Understanding human behaviors and needs more effectively can positively shape both individual lives and societal structures. However, individual rights and ethical principles must not be overlooked in this process.

Artificial intelligence and machine learning have made the analysis of human data faster and more efficient. Algorithms extract meaningful insights from large datasets, aiding decision-making processes. However, ensuring these technologies remain unbiased and free from prejudices is essential.

In conclusion, the collection and analysis of human data present both opportunities and responsibilities. While technological advancements make these processes more powerful and effective, ethical and security considerations are critical to ensuring the sustainable development of these technologies. Effectively utilizing human data can contribute to building a better future for individuals and societies alike.

3.2.1. Social Media, Biometric Data, and Daily Digital Footprints

Social media, biometric data, and daily digital footprints have become integral aspects of modern life. People generate vast amounts of data through their daily interactions on digital platforms. This data creates a digital footprint that provides deep insights into individual behaviors, preferences, and identities. However, this phenomenon presents significant opportunities while raising ethical and privacy concerns.

Social media is not just a platform for sharing thoughts and emotions; it is also a major source of data generation. Users' likes, comments, shares, and interactions reflect their interests, political views, and even moods. This data holds immense value for companies and researchers but also poses threats to individual privacy.

Biometric data refers to information derived from individuals' physical and behavioral traits. Fingerprints, facial recognition, voice patterns, eye movements, and even walking styles are examples of biometric data widely used in authentication and security processes. These data points are unique to individuals but carry significant risks if mishandled.

Daily digital footprints consist of the data fragments left behind as people browse the internet, use apps, or interact with digital devices. Examples include web browsing histories, shopping preferences, GPS location data, and device usage patterns. These footprints can be used to map individuals' movements and behaviors in detail.

When combined, these three types of data become powerful tools for building digital profiles. For instance, social media data can reveal a person's interests, biometric data can verify their identity, and digital footprints can illustrate their daily habits. This information is used in personalized marketing campaigns, security systems, and healthcare applications.

However, the collection and use of this data raise serious ethical concerns. Collecting data without individuals' knowledge or consent can lead to privacy breaches and data security risks. Sensitive data such as biometric information is particularly vulnerable to cyberattacks and malicious exploitation.

The commercial use of data has become increasingly common through social media and digital platforms. For example, social media platforms analyze user behavior to deliver targeted advertisements to advertisers. However, this practice can negatively impact user privacy and question their rights over their data.

Biometric data has revolutionized security technologies but has also raised concerns about constant surveillance. Facial recognition technologies can enhance public safety in crowded areas but, if misused, can restrict individual freedoms and become tools for societal control.

Digital footprints can improve user experiences and provide personalized services. For example, an e-commerce platform can analyze a user's past purchases to recommend relevant products. However, such applications increase the potential for data misuse and unauthorized sharing of users' information.

The management of such data requires legal and regulatory frameworks. Laws like the European Union's General Data Protection Regulation (GDPR) aim to give individuals more control over their data. However, implementing such regulations globally remains a challenge.

Transparent data collection and usage practices are critical to building trust among individuals. Users should be informed about what data is being collected and how it is being used. They should also have the right to protect and limit the sharing of their data.

Technology companies must take responsibility for managing this data ethically. By prioritizing user privacy in their policies, companies can ensure the security and confidentiality of personal information. Implementing security measures like data encryption and anonymization is also crucial.

In conclusion, social media, biometric data, and daily digital footprints are essential components of modern life, offering both significant opportunities and responsibilities. Fully leveraging the potential of this data requires a strong focus on ethics, security, and privacy. Striking a balance between protecting individuals' rights and reaping the benefits of technology is the key to a sustainable digital age.

3.2.2. Using These Data to Copy Personality

Copying personality involves the complex process of replicating an individual's thoughts, emotions, and behaviors within a digital system. Social media, biometric data, and daily digital footprints play a critical role in this process. These data sources, reflecting different aspects of human life, form the foundation for personality replication technologies.

Social media data provides a powerful resource for understanding an individual's personality. Likes, shares, comments, and other activities on social media reveal their interests, values, and social behaviors. For instance, the type of content someone frequently shares can offer valuable insights into their worldview and personal preferences.

Biometric data helps analyze the physical and behavioral dimensions of personality. For example, facial expressions and voice tones can provide insights into an individual's emotional states. Such data is essential for modeling a person's emotional intelligence and reactions. Moreover, biometric data forms the foundation for digitally recreating an individual's unique traits.

Daily digital footprints, such as internet browsing history, shopping preferences, and GPS location data, reflect a person's lifestyle and habits, contributing significantly to the personality replication process. For instance, the places an individual frequently visits can provide information about their hobbies and daily routines.

The collection and analysis of these data allow artificial intelligence algorithms to be trained for personality replication. Machine learning and deep learning models identify patterns within these data, creating a digital model that represents the individual's personality traits. This enables the development of artificial systems that imitate the unique characteristics of the individual.

Analyzing social media data plays a significant role in understanding an individual's social interactions and relationships. For example, the connections a person forms through social media reveal their social network and interaction style. This information can be used to model their social intelligence and communication skills.

Biometric data is particularly valuable for understanding emotional states and reactions. For instance, facial recognition technologies can analyze an individual's emotional response to a situation. Such insights can add an emotional dimension to a digital personality model.

Digital footprints help uncover behavioral patterns. For example, an individual's shopping history reflects their economic preferences and consumption habits. This data can be used to replicate decision-making mechanisms in a digital system.

The data used in personality replication not only reflects an individual's current state but can also predict future behaviors. Artificial intelligence algorithms analyze past behaviors to forecast how the individual might make decisions in the future, adding a dynamic aspect to personality replication.

Combining these data sources allows for the creation of a more comprehensive digital portrait of the individual. Social media data, biometric data, and digital footprints together help understand and model the complex structure of thoughts, emotions, and behaviors.

However, ethical and privacy concerns are paramount in this process. Collecting data without individuals' consent can lead to privacy breaches and trust issues. Furthermore, the misuse of this data increases risks related to identity theft and security.

The accuracy and impartiality of the data used in personality replication are also critical factors. Errors or biases in the data can hinder the creation of an accurate digital model. Therefore, careful analysis and processing of data are essential.

This technology also holds great potential for medical applications. For instance, personality replication technologies can help monitor mental health and understand emotional states. In conditions like Alzheimer's, preserving an individual's memories and personality traits digitally could provide support for patients and their families.

The personality replication process can offer applications that simplify individuals' lives. For instance, a digital assistant that learns a person's personality traits can provide a more personalized experience. However, protecting individuals' rights and ensuring ethical standards is essential in this process.

In conclusion, social media, biometric data, and digital footprints are fundamental resources for personality replication. The integration and analysis of these data sources make it possible to digitally recreate an individual's thoughts, emotions, and behaviors. However, addressing ethical, security, and privacy concerns is crucial for the responsible development of this technology.

3.3. THE DIGITAL REPLICATION PROCESS: ARTIFICIAL INTELLIGENCE ALGORITHMS

The digital replication process involves recreating an individual's thoughts, emotions, and behaviors within a digital system using artificial intelligence (AI) algorithms. This process is made possible through the integration of advanced technologies such as big data analytics, machine learning, and deep learning. Digitally representing human traits showcases both the complexity and power of AI algorithms.

AI algorithms serve as the cornerstone of the digital replication process. These algorithms extract insights from the data generated by individuals and use them to develop systems that model their unique characteristics. For example, social media activity, biometric data, and digital footprints are among the data sources used to train these algorithms.

Machine learning algorithms are utilized in the digital replication process to analyze behavioral patterns. These algorithms review past data to predict an individual's future decisions and reactions. For instance, a system that learns a person's preferences can more accurately anticipate their next steps.

Deep learning enables more complex data analysis within the digital replication process. Leveraging artificial neural networks, deep learning models can better understand an individual's emotional responses, thoughts, and behaviors. Techniques like facial recognition and natural language processing (NLP) are critical components of this process.

AI algorithms also model emotional intelligence in the personality replication process. Algorithms analyze emotional indicators such as facial expressions, voice tones, and word choices to replicate these attributes in a digital model. This allows digital replicas to behave more human-like.

Data analytics plays a significant role in fueling AI algorithms within the digital replication process. Algorithms identify patterns and relationships within large datasets to define the unique traits of an individual. This process requires careful data cleaning and preprocessing to ensure accuracy.

Natural Language Processing (NLP) is another AI technique used to help digital replicas understand and produce human language. NLP algorithms analyze written and spoken expressions to model an individual's communication style and linguistic preferences. This enables digital replicas to interact with humans more naturally and effectively.

Ethical challenges significantly shape how AI algorithms are applied in the digital replication process. It is crucial for algorithms to remain unbiased and protect individual privacy. Poorly trained or biased algorithms can negatively impact the accuracy and authenticity of a person's digital replica.

Security measures play a vital role in protecting the digital models created by AI algorithms. Techniques such as data encryption and identity verification must be implemented to prevent digital replicas from being misused or compromised.

In conclusion, the digital replication process highlights the strength and sophistication of artificial intelligence algorithms. These algorithms learn from individuals' data to recreate their thoughts, emotions, and behaviors within a digital model. However, ensuring ethical and security standards is critical to responsibly harnessing this transformative technology.

3.3.1. Analysis of Personal Data

The analysis of personal data is a process used to understand individuals' behaviors, preferences, and lifestyles. This involves interpreting large amounts of data collected through digital devices, social media, biometric systems, and daily activities. Rapid advancements in technology have made personal data analysis more effective, while also raising significant privacy and ethical concerns

Personal data analysis typically involves examining demographic, behavioral, and biometric data. Demographic data reflects basic information such as age, gender, and education level. Behavioral data includes shopping habits, web browsing history, and social media interactions, while biometric data encompasses physical traits and biological markers.

The analysis of this data is carried out using advanced technologies such as artificial intelligence and machine learning. Algorithms identify patterns and trends within large datasets to predict behaviors and needs. For example, an e-commerce platform can analyze a user's purchase history to provide personalized product recommendations.

The healthcare sector is one of the most effective users of personal data analysis. Patients' biometric and medical data can be analyzed to enable early diagnosis of diseases and optimize treatment plans. Additionally, data analytics can monitor mental health conditions and create personalized therapy strategies.

In marketing, personal data analysis is a critical tool for understanding target audiences and developing effective strategies. Companies analyze consumer preferences to create more specific and impactful advertising campaigns. However, this process must carefully address potential impacts on individuals' privacy.

In education, personal data analysis is used to create personalized learning experiences by analyzing students' learning habits and performance. These analyses help identify students' strengths and weaknesses, enabling a more effective educational process.

Personal data analysis can also improve everyday services. For instance, smart city projects use behavioral data to enhance traffic management, energy consumption, and public services. However, transparency in how this data is collected and used is essential to maintain public trust.

Another critical application of this process is in security. Biometric data is used for authentication and access control. However, analyzing and storing such data must involve robust security measures, as biometric data is highly sensitive and vulnerable to identity theft.

Ethical considerations play a significant role in personal data analysis. Collecting data without individuals' consent can lead to privacy violations and trust issues. Therefore, obtaining consent and ensuring transparency in data collection and analysis processes is fundamental.

In data analysis processes, it is essential to properly clean and process the data. Errors or gaps in raw data can negatively impact the accuracy of analysis results. Additionally, ensuring that algorithms operate without bias is critical for obtaining reliable outcomes.

Today, personal data analysis has become faster and more scalable thanks to big data technologies and cloud computing infrastructures. This enables the processing of vast amounts of data to deliver more effective solutions tailored to individual needs.

However, privacy and security standards must be maintained in the use of these technologies.

In conclusion, the analysis of personal data is a powerful tool for understanding individuals' behaviors and needs. This process offers significant benefits in fields such as healthcare, education, marketing, and security. However, without attention to ethics, privacy, and data security, the use of these technologies could jeopardize individuals' rights and privacy. Therefore, it is crucial to carry out personal data analysis responsibly.

3.3.2. The Ability of Algorithms to Learn and Simulate Personality Traits

Algorithms have become increasingly capable of learning and simulating human behavior and personality traits. Using artificial intelligence (AI) and machine learning techniques, they analyze vast amounts of data to understand thought patterns, emotions, and behavioral tendencies. This capability is a significant step toward both understanding individuals and creating their digital replicas

Machine learning algorithms analyze behavioral data to uncover personality traits. For instance, data sources such as social media activity, shopping preferences, or facial expressions can provide insights into fundamental personality characteristics like introversion, extroversion, or emotional stability. This analysis is made possible through the integration of psychology and data science.

As algorithms learn personality traits, they identify patterns within large datasets. Deep learning techniques, utilizing complex neural networks, enable more sophisticated analysis of an individual's thought processes and emotional states. For example, facial recognition and natural language processing methods can model a person's real-time emotional responses and communication style.

These algorithms are not only capable of learning personality traits but also simulating them. Simulation involves reproducing an individual's thoughts and behaviors within a digital environment. For example, an AI system can mimic a person's writing style, speech patterns, or decision-making processes. This ability has applications in digital assistants and customer service technologies.

Personality simulation allows algorithms to create human-like interactions. This is particularly advantageous in applications such as social robots and virtual assistants. For instance, an AI-powered robot can provide more natural and effective interactions by responding appropriately to an individual's emotional states.

However, the ability of algorithms to learn and simulate personality traits raises ethical and privacy concerns. Collecting data without individuals' consent can lead to privacy violations and increase security risks. It is therefore essential to develop algorithms transparently and responsibly, ensuring that they respect individual rights and privacy.

In conclusion, the ability of algorithms to learn and simulate personality traits is a powerful tool for understanding human behavior and reproducing it in digital systems. While these technologies enhance the effectiveness of AI applications, they also require a cautious approach to address ethical, security, and privacy issues. These evolving capabilities have the potential to transform the relationship between humans and machines.

3.4. TRANSFERRING MEMORY, EMOTIONS, AND THOUGHTS TO ARTIFICIAL INTELLIGENCE

The transfer of memory, emotions, and thoughts to artificial intelligence (AI) involves the process of recreating human experiences and internal processes in a digital system. This ambitious endeavor aims to enable AI systems to understand and replicate human cognition and emotions. The transfer of memory and emotions to AI is not just a technical innovation but also raises profound ethical and philosophical questions about the essence of being human.

Memory transfer involves the digital recording and processing of an individual's experiences, knowledge, and recollections. This process is made possible through brain-computer interfaces and advanced data analytics. For instance, data representing significant events in an individual's life can be integrated into an AI model to digitally recreate their memory.

The transfer of memories requires the digitization of neural processes. Neural connections and electrical activities in the human brain determine how memories are formed and stored. Artificial neural networks aim to model these processes, striving to understand and replicate the past experiences of individuals.

Emotion transfer is a critical component of enabling AI to interact in a human-like manner. Human emotions are expressed through various indicators such as facial expressions, tone of voice, and body language. AI systems analyze these indicators to interpret an individual's emotional states. For example, AI technologies capable of recognizing happiness, sadness, or anger through facial expressions have already been developed.

The digitization of emotional states allows AI to behave in ways that feel more human. For example, a virtual assistant can analyze a user's emotional state and respond with empathy, providing a more personalized and engaging experience. This enhances the natural interaction between AI and humans.

The transfer of thoughts to AI involves understanding an individual's mental processes and recreating them in a digital model. Brain imaging technologies and artificial neural networks are used to analyze thoughts and represent them digitally. This enables AI to model cognitive abilities such as problem-solving, decision-making, and creativity.

The transfer of memory, emotions, and thoughts to AI has significant potential in the healthcare sector. For example, digitally preserving memories could help Alzheimer's patients regain access to their lost recollections. Additionally, this technology can be used in therapeutic applications to assist individuals in processing and overcoming traumatic experiences.

This technology also has transformative applications in education. The digitization of memory and thought processes enables the creation of personalized learning programs. For instance, an AI system that analyzes a student's learning habits could recommend the most effective strategies for their educational development.

However, transferring memory, emotions, and thoughts to AI raises ethical and privacy concerns. Collecting such data without individuals' consent can lead to privacy violations. Additionally, the misuse of this data poses risks to individuals' identity and security.

Another critical aspect of this process is the accuracy and impartiality of the data. For memory and thought processes to be accurately digitized, the data must be processed without errors or biases. Otherwise, the digital models created by AI may fail to reflect the true characteristics of the individual.

The ability of AI to simulate emotions and thoughts represents not only a technical milestone but also a transformation that questions the meaning of being human. If an AI system can successfully replicate all emotional and cognitive traits of an individual, should it be considered an extension of the individual or an entirely independent entity? This question could shape the future development of AI technologies.

In conclusion, transferring memory, emotions, and thoughts to artificial intelligence represents a significant leap in understanding and recreating the human mind. While this process enhances the capabilities of AI applications, it also sparks deep discussions about ethics, privacy, and human identity. Advances in this area will create new opportunities and challenges at both individual and societal levels.

3.4.1. Building the Digital Soul: Transferring Human Thought to Artificial Intelligence

The concept of building a digital soul involves transferring human thoughts, emotions, and mental processes into artificial intelligence (AI). This process aims to reconstruct the complexity of the human mind in a digital model, enabling an artificial system to exhibit human-like consciousness and behavior. The development of such technologies sparks scientific and philosophical debates about the nature of humanity and the essence of being human.

Transferring human thought to AI first requires a deep understanding of how mental processes work. The human brain is a complex system that processes information through neural connections and electrical activities. Mimicking these mechanisms in a digital environment is made possible by technologies such as artificial neural networks and deep learning algorithms.

The process of thought transfer involves collecting and analyzing vast amounts of data about individuals' mental processes. This includes behaviors, written and spoken expressions, decision-making mechanisms, and problem-solving skills. These data are critical for training AI systems to model human thought.

Natural Language Processing (NLP) plays a significant role in transferring human thought to AI. NLP algorithms analyze individuals' word choices, language structures, and communication styles to model their ways of thinking. This allows AI to replicate the linguistic and cognitive characteristics of individuals.

Emotional processes are another critical component of building a digital soul. Human thoughts are often shaped and guided by emotions. AI systems can analyze emotional states through facial expressions, tone of voice, and other biometric indicators, using this information to generate human-like responses.

The concept of the digital soul also encompasses personal identity and self-awareness. This requires recreating an individual's past experiences, values, and beliefs in a digital system. The digitization of memories, emotions, and thoughts makes it possible to create a "digital twin" of a person.

Building a digital soul holds transformative potential in healthcare. For example, AI-assisted therapeutic systems could be developed for individuals with mental health challenges. Additionally, preserving the memories of elderly individuals digitally could help compensate for memory loss caused by aging or conditions like Alzheimer's.

In education, the digital soul concept can be used to understand student performance and learning habits. AI can analyze students' thought processes and recommend the most effective learning strategies, providing a more personalized and impactful educational experience.

However, transferring human thought to AI raises ethical and philosophical concerns. Digitizing a person's mental processes could lead to privacy violations and spark debates about identity rights. Additionally, the existence of a digital soul may redefine the meaning of being human.

Technological limitations also pose a significant challenge in building a digital soul. Fully understanding the complexity of the human brain and recreating it in a digital model requires knowledge that surpasses current technological capabilities. Progress in this field depends on both scientific and technical innovations.

The construction of a digital soul also has the potential to transform the relationship between humans and machines. Digitizing human thoughts can enable AI systems to operate more closely and effectively with humans. However, this advancement also calls for the establishment of new ethical boundaries in human-machine interactions.

The ability of an AI system to fully simulate human thought raises questions about whether the system is an extension of the individual or an independent entity. This will be a critical topic of discussion shaping how digital souls are perceived at both individual and societal levels.

In conclusion, building a digital soul expands the technological boundaries of humanity through the transfer of human thought to artificial intelligence. This process represents not only a scientific achievement but also an ethical, philosophical, and societal transformation. Recreating the human mind in a digital form has the potential to reshape both individual lives and societal structures in profound ways.

3.4.2. Formation of Mental and Emotional Representations

Mental and emotional representations are the result of an individual's processes for perceiving, understanding, and responding to environmental stimuli. These representations serve as internal models that allow the human mind to organize and make sense of information and emotions. Formed by the interplay of cognitive and emotional processes, these representations are fundamental to human experience.

Mental representations enable individuals to comprehend and organize the world around them. These models, which represent objects, events, or concepts, start with perception and are enriched by information stored in memory. For example, an individual's mental representation of a "table" is shaped by the table's physical characteristics, function, and prior experiences with similar objects.

Emotional representations, on the other hand, regulate an individual's emotional states and responses. An emotion may arise from a specific event and is then interpreted through mental representations. For instance, a teddy bear for a child might represent feelings of safety and happiness. Such representations develop over time through an individual's emotional experiences.

Mental and emotional representations are formed through neural connections in the human brain. Neural networks encode the experiences individuals have and create associations between them. Memory serves as the repository where these representations are stored and retrieved when needed.

Sensory input plays a critical role in the formation of mental and emotional representations. Everything an individual sees, hears, or touches contributes to the construction of these representations. For example, a pleasant fragrance might evoke a happy memory from the past in an individual's mind. This process engages both cognitive and emotional learning mechanisms.

These representations play a significant role in guiding behavior. They influence how individuals perceive situations, how they feel about them, and how they respond. For example, when confronted with danger, a fear representation is activated, prompting the individual to take actions like fleeing or defending themselves.

Representations also shape social interactions between individuals. Emotional representations developed through interactions with others can influence expectations in future relationships. For example, an individual with a representation of distrust may approach new relationships with caution.

Mental and emotional representations also hold great potential in artificial intelligence applications. Artificial neural networks and deep learning algorithms can model these human brain processes to create more human-like artificial systems. Emotional intelligence in AI systems, for instance, could analyze such representations to communicate more effectively and naturally with individuals.

However, artificially recreating these representations presents both technical and ethical challenges. The complexity of emotional processes in the human brain and the diversity of individual experiences make it difficult to fully simulate these representations. Additionally, ensuring privacy and adhering to ethical standards are significant responsibilities in developing such technologies.

In conclusion, mental and emotional representations are fundamental processes that enable individuals to perceive, interpret, and interact with the world. These representations are critical for understanding human behavior and developing artificial systems. However, the complexity and depth of these processes require careful consideration in both research and technological applications.

4. INTEGRATION OF HUMAN PERSONALITY WITH HUMANOID ROBOTS

The integration of human personality with humanoid robots represents a significant advancement in technology's ability to mimic human behavior and emotions. This process involves representing human personality in a digital system and embedding it into humanoid robots. As a result, robots transition from being purely mechanical tools to entities capable of exhibiting human-like behaviors.

Integrating human personality into humanoid robots requires the incorporation of emotional intelligence and social interaction capabilities. This enables robots to understand human emotions, respond appropriately, and communicate naturally with people. For instance, a robot could detect if someone is feeling sad and provide supportive responses.

This process involves artificial intelligence (AI) systems learning personality traits and integrating them into robotic behaviors. AI algorithms can analyze individuals' social media interactions, communication styles, and other digital footprints to model their communication and decision-making patterns. This allows humanoid robots to deliver more personalized services to individuals.

The integration of human personality with humanoid robots holds great potential, particularly in caregiving and healthcare services. Humanoid robots designed for elderly individuals or people living alone can provide not only physical assistance but also emotional support. For example, a robot could analyze a person's mood and engage in conversations that uplift their spirits.

In the education sector, humanoid robots can offer tailored learning experiences based on students' individual learning styles. Robots can analyze students' needs and strengths, enhancing their performance. Additionally, robots have the potential to assist teachers by providing individualized guidance and support to students.

However, integrating human personality with humanoid robots raises ethical and privacy concerns. Representing human personality in a digital system necessitates safeguarding personal data and preventing its misuse. Additionally, there are ongoing discussions about the psychological effects of robots on humans and the boundaries of human-robot relationships.

The ability of robots to mimic real human behavior brings up questions about whether they should be considered tools or independent entities. If humanoid robots successfully integrate human personalities, this could fundamentally alter human-machine interactions and create a new social dynamic.

In conclusion, the integration of human personality with humanoid robots is a technological innovation that represents the capacity to mimic and enhance human experiences. This process has the potential to revolutionize fields such as healthcare, education, and social services. However, ethical, privacy, and societal implications must be carefully addressed in the development of this technology. Clearly defining the boundaries of human-robot relationships will be critical to ensuring the responsible and sustainable use of humanoid robots.

4.1. HUMANOID ROBOTS AND TECHNOLOGICAL INFRASTRUCTURE

Humanoid robots are advanced systems designed to exhibit human-like physical and behavioral characteristics. These robots are not merely machines performing specific tasks but entities capable of interacting with humans and responding appropriately to environmental stimuli. Their effective functioning relies on a sophisticated technological infrastructure, which integrates innovations from multiple disciplines.

One of the most critical components of humanoid robots is artificial intelligence (AI). AI enables robots to perceive, analyze, and respond to environmental data. Deep learning algorithms, in particular, enhance the ability of robots to solve complex problems, understand human language, and learn continuously. This infrastructure allows humanoid robots to update and improve themselves over time.

On the hardware side, sensors and actuators play a vital role. Sensors allow robots to collect environmental data, including visual, auditory, tactile, and even thermal information. These inputs help robots interact with humans more naturally. Actuators, on the other hand, enable robots to execute movements based on this data, making human-like gestures and expressions possible.

Another crucial component of the technological infrastructure for humanoid robots is natural language processing (NLP) systems. NLP allows robots to understand and generate human language. By analyzing text and speech data, NLP enables robots to communicate more naturally with humans. This capability makes humanoid robots effective in applications ranging from customer service to education.

Advanced robotic systems also require mechanical designs for movement and balance. The ability of humanoid robots to mimic human anatomy and movement relies on mechanical components supported by complex algorithms. These robots can simulate human motions such as walking, running, or grasping objects with remarkable precision.

Cloud computing is another integral part of the technological infrastructure for humanoid robots. Cloud-based systems provide robots with access to extensive data sources and the ability to learn from them. Moreover, cloud infrastructure allows robots to overcome hardware limitations and perform more complex tasks.

The development of humanoid robots also depends on advancements in energy management and battery technologies. These robots require efficient energy usage to operate for extended periods. Advanced battery systems and energy management solutions enable humanoid robots to have longer operational lifespans and greater mobility.

Ethics and safety are significant aspects of the technological infrastructure of humanoid robots. These robots must interact with humans safely and respect their privacy. As a result, programming humanoid robots must adhere to strict safety standards and ethical principles to ensure responsible use.

In conclusion, humanoid robots are made possible through the convergence of technologies such as artificial intelligence, sensors, natural language processing, mechanical designs, and cloud computing. This infrastructure allows robots to function not only as practical tools but also as systems capable of human-like interactions. However, ethical considerations and safety measures are essential to ensure the responsible and sustainable development and deployment of humanoid robots.

4.1.1. The Development of Humanoid Robots: Physical and Emotional Interaction

The development of humanoid robots has evolved significantly, with a focus on enabling both physical and emotional interaction with humans. These robots are designed to not only perform tasks but also engage with individuals in a way that mimics human behavior and emotions. This dual focus on physical and emotional capabilities marks a transformative shift in robotics, creating machines that can effectively integrate into human environments.

Physical interaction is one of the foundational aspects of humanoid robot development. Robots are equipped with advanced mechanical systems that replicate human-like movements such as walking, running, lifting, and precise manipulation of objects. These capabilities are made possible by sophisticated actuators, sensors, and control algorithms that allow for smooth and coordinated actions.

A critical aspect of physical interaction is safety. Humanoid robots are often designed with materials and control systems that minimize the risk of harm during human-robot interactions. For example, soft robotics technologies ensure that robots can work alongside humans without causing injury, even in close-contact scenarios.

Humanoid robots are also advancing in their ability to navigate and adapt to complex environments. Equipped with sensors such as LiDAR, cameras, and accelerometers, these robots can perceive their surroundings and make real-time adjustments to their movements. This capability enables them to operate in dynamic spaces, such as homes, offices, or public areas.

Emotional interaction is equally critical in the development of humanoid robots. Emotional intelligence in robots involves the ability to recognize, interpret, and respond to human emotions. This is achieved through technologies like facial recognition, natural language processing (NLP), and voice tone analysis. These systems allow robots to detect emotional cues and adapt their behavior accordingly.

For instance, a humanoid robot interacting with a person who appears upset might respond with empathetic language or soothing gestures. Such emotional responsiveness enhances the user experience, making robots more relatable and effective in settings such as healthcare, therapy, and customer service.

Humanoid robots are increasingly used in healthcare for emotional support. For example, robots can assist elderly individuals by providing companionship, reminding them to take medication, or engaging them in stimulating conversations. Emotional interaction in these scenarios can reduce feelings of loneliness and improve overall well-being.

In education, humanoid robots are being developed to create more engaging learning experiences. These robots can adjust their teaching styles based on the emotional and cognitive needs of students. For example, a robot might offer encouragement to a struggling student or use humor to maintain engagement during a lesson.

The integration of physical and emotional interaction capabilities in humanoid robots also extends to entertainment and social applications. Robots designed for these purposes can entertain audiences, host events, or serve as interactive companions, enhancing human experiences in creative ways.

Despite these advancements, the development of humanoid robots faces significant challenges. Creating robots capable of genuine emotional understanding remains a complex task due to the intricacies of human emotions. Similarly, ensuring that physical interactions are safe and intuitive requires continuous innovation in hardware and software.

Ethical concerns also arise in the development of humanoid robots. Questions about the extent to which robots should mimic human emotions and behaviors are subjects of ongoing debate. Additionally, issues related to data privacy, user consent, and the psychological impact of human-robot relationships must be carefully addressed.

Another challenge is the accessibility of humanoid robots. The advanced technologies required for physical and emotional interaction often make these robots expensive, limiting their availability to select industries or individuals. Reducing costs while maintaining functionality is a key goal for developers.

Public perception plays a significant role in the acceptance of humanoid robots. For robots to be widely adopted, they must overcome societal skepticism and fears about automation. Designing robots that are approachable, trustworthy, and aligned with human values is essential for building public confidence.

In conclusion, the development of humanoid robots is advancing rapidly, focusing on enhancing both physical and emotional interaction. These robots have the potential to revolutionize fields such as healthcare, education, and entertainment by providing innovative solutions to human needs. However, addressing technical, ethical, and societal challenges is essential to ensure the responsible and inclusive evolution of this transformative technology.

4.1.3. Integration of Robotic Technology with Artificial Intelligence

The integration of robotic technology with artificial intelligence (AI) represents a groundbreaking transformation in modern engineering and science. This convergence enables robots to become smarter, more autonomous, and better suited to meet human needs. AI provides robotic systems with not only mechanical functionality but also the ability to make decisions, learn, and adapt to changing environments.

AI-powered robots possess the capability to collect and analyze environmental data. AI algorithms process data from sensors, allowing robots to understand their surroundings and develop appropriate responses in real-time. For example, an industrial robot can detect the exact position of materials on a production line and handle them with precision.

Machine learning plays a critical role in the integration of robotic technology with AI. This technology allows robots to learn from past experiences and improve their performance in future tasks. For instance, a cleaning robot can analyze usage patterns to identify high-traffic areas and optimize its cleaning routines accordingly.

Deep learning enhances the ability of robots to perform more complex tasks. Techniques such as image recognition, object detection, and natural language processing (NLP) enable robots to interact with their environments more naturally. For example, a service robot can understand spoken language and respond appropriately to user queries.

The integration of robotic systems with AI strengthens human-robot collaboration. While traditional robots excel in repetitive and predictable tasks, AI-powered robots can operate in more dynamic and complex environments. For example, robots in healthcare can assist surgeons with precision during surgeries.

This integration has also revolutionized industrial manufacturing. In smart factories, AI-enabled robots optimize production processes, increasing efficiency. These robots can predict equipment failures and identify maintenance needs in advance, minimizing production downtime.

In agriculture, the integration of robotics with AI facilitates the development of smart farming practices. For instance, AI-powered agricultural robots can monitor crop health, detect pests, and perform precise irrigation or fertilization. This improves agricultural productivity while promoting sustainable resource use.

The impact of this integration is also evident in education and social services. AI-enabled robots can provide individualized learning support to students and offer social interaction for elderly individuals. For example, an educational robot can adapt to a student's learning pace and deliver customized content to enhance engagement and comprehension.

The integration of robotics and AI has significant potential in logistics and transportation as well. Autonomous vehicles and delivery robots use AI algorithms to analyze traffic conditions, plan optimal routes, and navigate safely to their destinations.

However, this integration also raises numerous technical and ethical challenges. Robots controlled by AI bring up issues related to data privacy, security, and autonomy. Specifically, the ability of robots to make independent decisions prompts debates about accountability and responsibility for those decisions.

Security measures are critical in the integration of robotics with AI. Robust protocols must be implemented to protect systems from cyberattacks and ensure safe interaction with humans. Additionally, these technologies must be developed and deployed in compliance with ethical principles.

In conclusion, the integration of robotic technology with artificial intelligence offers innovative solutions across various sectors, transforming human life in profound ways. However, successful and sustainable implementation requires addressing technical, ethical, and societal challenges. This transformation marks a new era in human-robot interaction and reshapes both industrial and everyday life.

4.2. TRANSFERRING DIGITAL PERSONALITY TO ROBOTIC SYSTEMS

The transfer of digital personality to robotic systems involves integrating a digital model of an individual's thoughts, emotions, and behaviors into humanoid robots. This process enables robots to transition from being purely mechanical devices to entities capable of exhibiting human-like interaction and personality traits. Representing human personality in a digital system is made possible through the convergence of artificial intelligence (AI), machine learning, and robotics technology.

A digital personality is constructed using data from an individual's social media interactions, written and spoken expressions, behavioral patterns, and biometric information. This data is processed by AI algorithms to create a model that reflects the individual's unique characteristics and preferences. When integrated into robotic systems, this model allows robots to exhibit responses and behaviors that align with the individual's personality.

One of the critical aspects of this technology is the ability of robots to understand emotional states and respond appropriately. Emotional cues such as facial expressions, tone of voice, and speech patterns enable robots to analyze a person's mood. For instance, a humanoid robot could detect sadness in a person and respond with empathetic language and comforting gestures.

Transferring digital personality to robotic systems enables robots to communicate in a more human-like manner. This capability offers significant advantages in sectors such as customer service, education, and healthcare. For example, a healthcare robot could use a personalized personality model to understand a patient's needs and provide both practical assistance and emotional support.

This process requires strict adherence to data privacy and ethical standards. The data used to create digital personalities must be collected and processed with the individual's consent. Additionally, robust security measures are essential to prevent misuse of the data. Ensuring privacy is critical for the public acceptance of this technology.

Robots with integrated digital personalities can offer highly personalized experiences. For instance, an educational robot could adapt its teaching methods to suit a student's learning pace and style, making the education process more effective and individualized.

In the healthcare sector, robots with digital personalities can provide emotional support for elderly individuals. These robots can analyze a person's past experiences and preferences to foster meaningful interactions. For example, a robot could play a person's favorite music or engage in conversations about cherished memories, reducing feelings of loneliness.

Integrating digital personalities into robotic systems can also enhance the social acceptance of humanoid robots. Robots capable of human-like responses and understanding individual needs are likely to be perceived as more approachable and trustworthy, paving the way for a new era of human-robot interaction.

However, ethical questions remain a significant consideration in the development of this technology. Debates continue about the extent to which robots should mimic human personalities and where the boundaries should be drawn. The psychological impact of human-like robots on individuals must also be carefully evaluated.

In conclusion, transferring digital personality to robotic systems is an innovative advancement that allows robots to work more harmoniously and effectively with humans. This technology has the potential to revolutionize fields such as healthcare, education, and social services. However, its responsible development requires careful attention to ethical, privacy, and societal considerations. With these safeguards in place, robots with digital personalities can become tools that simplify and enrich human lives.

4.2.1. Learning Capacities of Robots with Artificial Intelligence

Robots equipped with artificial intelligence (AI) are becoming increasingly advanced in their learning capacities. These robots can collect and analyze environmental data, use it to improve their performance, and apply what they learn to future tasks. Their learning capabilities are supported by technologies such as machine learning, deep learning, and data processing.

Machine learning is a fundamental technology that enables robots to learn from experience. With this technology, robots can optimize their performance by repeatedly executing specific tasks. For instance, an industrial robot can analyze its mistakes and improve its efficiency in assembly processes over time.

Deep learning allows robots to perform more complex learning tasks. Based on artificial neural networks, this technology enables robots to carry out high-level cognitive functions such as image recognition, object detection, and speech comprehension. For example, a delivery robot can identify obstacles in its path and calculate alternative routes.

AI-powered robots do not solely rely on environmental data for learning; they can also learn from interactions with humans. Technologies like natural language processing (NLP) and emotional analysis enable robots to understand user needs and emotional states through communication. This allows robots to provide more personalized and human-like services.

Robots' learning capacities also enhance their adaptability. To handle dynamic and changing environments, robots use learning algorithms to adjust to new situations. For example, a household cleaning robot can create a new cleaning route when furniture is rearranged.

AI-equipped robots can continuously update and improve themselves through their learning capabilities. This process is supported by cloud computing technologies. Robots can access extensive data resources via the cloud, share information with other robots, and engage in collective learning. This significantly increases their learning speed and capacity.

In healthcare, robots with advanced learning capacities have significant potential. For instance, surgical robots can learn from the commands given by surgeons during operations to perform more precise and reliable interventions. Additionally, AI-powered rehabilitation robots can analyze patients' recovery processes and develop more effective treatment methods.

In education, robots with AI-driven learning capacities can offer personalized teaching methods tailored to individual students' needs. These robots can analyze students' learning speeds and preferences, providing materials that address their strengths and weaknesses. This makes the education process more efficient and effective.

However, the learning capacities of robots raise ethical and security concerns. Protecting the privacy of the data collected by robots and ensuring its proper use are critical for gaining user trust. Moreover, maintaining control over robots' autonomous learning processes is essential to prevent unintended outcomes.

The economic and societal impacts of robots' learning capacities must also be carefully assessed. While these robots can increase efficiency and reduce costs, they may also lead to the automation of certain jobs. Therefore, the impact of AI-powered robots on the workforce should be analyzed thoroughly.

In conclusion, the learning capacities of robots with artificial intelligence are driving a significant transformation in technology. These robots provide solutions that simplify and enrich human lives through their continuous learning and adaptability. However, ethical, security, and societal implications must be addressed carefully to ensure responsible and sustainable development of this technology.

4.2.2. The Role of Humanoid Robots in Personality and Consciousness Simulation

Humanoid robots play a crucial role in the simulation of personality and consciousness, standing at the forefront of efforts to digitally recreate human minds and behaviors. These robots aim to establish natural and meaningful interactions by mimicking human behavior and emotional responses. Personality and consciousness simulation transforms humanoid robots from task-oriented devices into entities capable of human-like presence.

Personality simulation involves understanding and replicating individuals' personal traits and behavioral patterns. This is achieved through advanced data analytics powered by artificial intelligence (AI) and machine learning algorithms. Robots can model an individual's communication style and personality traits by learning from their social interactions, language usage, and behavioral data.

Consciousness simulation, however, is a more complex process. Consciousness is defined as an individual's ability to perceive their own existence and surroundings, encompassing self-awareness, reasoning, and decision-making. For humanoid robots to simulate consciousness, advanced artificial neural networks must integrate perception, learning, and decision-making processes.

Humanoid robots can recognize emotional states by analyzing facial expressions, vocal tones, and language patterns. This highlights the critical role of emotional intelligence in personality and consciousness simulation. For example, a robot might detect sadness in a person and respond with empathetic language or comforting gestures. Such emotional responses deepen and enhance human-robot interactions.

Personality simulation improves the social adaptability of humanoid robots. By understanding emotional and social needs, robots can provide more personalized and effective services. For instance, an educational robot could adapt to a student's learning style to enhance their motivation and engagement.

Consciousness simulation enables robots to operate more independently and autonomously. This allows robots to handle complex tasks with greater flexibility and adaptability. For example, a healthcare robot could analyze a patient's medical condition and independently suggest appropriate interventions.

The role of humanoid robots in personality and consciousness simulation also has significant implications in caregiving. Robots designed for elderly care can use personality simulation to meet emotional needs and support daily activities. These robots can reduce feelings of loneliness and improve the quality of life for elderly individuals.

In education, robots with personality simulation can provide customized teaching materials tailored to students' individual needs. By analyzing students' strengths and weaknesses, these robots can optimize learning processes and support teachers in creating more effective educational environments.

However, the simulation of personality and consciousness by humanoid robots raises ethical and societal concerns. Questions about the extent to which robots should mimic human personalities and behaviors are subjects of ongoing debate. Furthermore, the psychological impact of human-like robots on individuals must be carefully examined.

Technological limitations pose significant challenges in the simulation of personality and consciousness. The complexity of human consciousness and the diversity of individual experiences can limit the accuracy of these simulations. Therefore, continuous research and innovation are essential to advance the capabilities of humanoid robots in this area.

Security and privacy are critical in the process of personality and consciousness simulation. Data collected by robots about individuals must be protected with stringent security protocols and used only for authorized purposes. Safeguarding privacy is essential not only to protect individuals but also to build trust in robotic systems.

Consciousness simulation could also enable robots to make ethical decisions. For instance, a social robot interacting with multiple individuals could evaluate the most appropriate response and act accordingly. Such capabilities allow robots to behave in ways that are more human-like and socially aware.

Personality and consciousness simulation could extend the role of humanoid robots to creative tasks. For example, a robot could adapt to an individual's artistic preferences and assist in areas like music or painting, or even generate new creative content.

In conclusion, the role of humanoid robots in personality and consciousness simulation represents a new era in human-machine interaction. These robots can better understand individual needs and provide more human-like and effective services. However, the development of this technology must address ethical, privacy, and societal considerations with a responsible approach.

Humanoid robots' role in simulating personality and consciousness has profound implications at both scientific and societal levels. This technology redefines the boundaries between humanity and technology, offering new opportunities and challenges in the digital future.

4.3. A NEW ERA IN HUMAN-ROBOT INTERACTION

Human-robot interaction has entered a new era with advancements in technology. Modern robots have evolved from simple mechanical devices into entities capable of communicating naturally with humans and adapting to their needs. The integration of artificial intelligence, machine learning, and emotional intelligence has revolutionized human-robot interaction, enabling deeper and more meaningful connections.

Today's robots are designed with the ability to understand human behavior and emotional states. Technologies such as facial recognition, natural language processing, and voice analysis allow robots to detect an individual's emotional condition and respond appropriately. For example, a robot can recognize sadness in a person and provide supportive and empathetic communication. This makes human-robot interactions more genuine and effective.

In this new era, robots are increasingly integrated into daily life in fields such as healthcare, education, and social services. In healthcare, robots can provide both physical and emotional support to elderly individuals, while in education, robots offer personalized learning experiences for students. These robots are no longer mere tools but companions that improve the quality of human life.

The advancements in human-robot interaction have also brought significant changes to the workplace. In industries like customer service and manufacturing, robots can collaborate effectively with humans to enhance efficiency. For example, a robot working in a store can answer customer inquiries and simplify the shopping experience.

However, this new era also raises ethical and societal questions. While robots' human-like behaviors foster trust and acceptance, they also blur the boundaries between humans and machines. Issues such as privacy and data security need to be carefully addressed to ensure responsible development and deployment of this technology.

As robots establish deeper connections with humans, their acceptance in society grows, but more research is needed to understand their psychological impacts. Long-term human-robot interactions, in particular, should be studied to evaluate their effects on social relationships and emotional well-being.

In conclusion, this new era in human-robot interaction enables technology to be used in more meaningful and beneficial ways for humans. While these advancements provide solutions that simplify, support, and enrich lives, they also bring ethical and societal challenges. Successfully navigating this era will require careful management of technological developments and alignment with human values to ensure a sustainable and harmonious integration of robots into society.

4.3.1. Emotional and Social Relationships with Robots Possessing Digital Personalities

Robots with digital personalities have the potential to establish meaningful and personalized emotional and social relationships with humans. By understanding individuals' behaviors, preferences, and emotional states, these robots make human-machine interactions more natural and effective. With the help of technologies such as artificial intelligence, natural language processing, and emotional analysis, robots can form deep connections with people.

Emotional relationships are one of the most striking aspects of robots with digital personalities. These robots can recognize and respond to emotional needs, offering support to individuals. For instance, a robot might engage in uplifting conversations with a person experiencing loneliness or provide companionship through meaningful interactions. This can serve as a valuable emotional support mechanism, especially for elderly individuals or those living alone.

The role of robots in social relationships lies in their ability to provide personalized interactions. A robot with a digital personality can analyze an individual's interests and past experiences to offer a tailored experience. For example, a robot could play a person's favorite music or discuss topics of mutual interest, creating a unique social bond.

These robots also have significant potential in therapeutic and caregiving settings. Robots designed for psychological support can analyze individuals' emotional states and respond appropriately to their needs. For instance, a robot could use a soothing tone to comfort someone under stress or offer calming suggestions.

In education, robots with digital personalities can enhance the learning process by adapting to students' emotional states. These robots can motivate students by recognizing their needs and offering personalized learning experiences. They can also help develop social skills and foster meaningful interactions with learners.

However, there are risks associated with forming emotional and social relationships with robots possessing digital personalities. People may become overly attached to these robots, potentially harming real human relationships. This risk is especially pronounced for individuals who are socially isolated, as they may become emotionally dependent on robots, exacerbating their isolation.

Privacy and security are critical considerations in relationships with robots. The personal data collected by robots about individuals must be protected and used solely for specific purposes. Ensuring data security and ethical practices will enhance users' trust in these technologies and mitigate potential concerns.

The development of emotional and social relationships with robots could also shift societal perceptions of these technologies. As people view robots with human-like traits, they may be more inclined to integrate them into their social environments. This trend could make human-robot relationships more common and acceptable in the future.

In conclusion, emotional and social relationships with robots possessing digital personalities open new doors in human-machine interaction. These robots can be effective tools for understanding emotional needs and providing social support. However, the societal impacts, ethical dimensions, and potential risks of such relationships must be carefully assessed. By addressing these factors, the responsible development and implementation of these technologies can ensure they enrich and support human lives in meaningful ways.

4.3.2. The Physical Features of Robots and Their Impact on Human Responses

The physical features of robots significantly influence the quality and nature of interactions they establish with humans. Humanoid robots, with their human-like appearances and movements, can create a more positive perception among people. Physical design plays a crucial role in ensuring robots are perceived as reliable, accessible, and effective companions.

Facial expressions and body language in humanoid robots enhance emotional interactions. When people see a facial expression on a robot, they are more likely to perceive it as "alive" and "empathetic." For example, a robot's smile can have a calming effect on users, making the interaction feel more genuine and friendly.

The size, color, and overall design of robots also shape human responses. Smaller, softer-featured robots are often seen as friendlier and less intimidating, particularly by children and elderly individuals. Conversely, larger, more robust robots are considered better suited for industrial or security purposes.

The fluidity and naturalness of movements deeply impact how robots are perceived. Robots capable of performing human-like motions are seen as more reliable and efficient assistants. For instance, a robot that can shake hands naturally can help foster a stronger connection with its user.

Touch-based interaction is another critical aspect of how robots influence human responses. Robots that provide a soft and reassuring sense of touch are more warmly received. This feature is particularly important in the design of healthcare and caregiving robots.

Voice tones and speech abilities also have as much influence as physical features on human responses. Robots with voices resembling human tones are considered more understandable and trustworthy. Additionally, an appropriate tone and rhythm in speech can add emotional depth to interactions.

The physical features of robots can also facilitate collaboration with humans. Ergonomic designs allow robots to perform specific tasks more efficiently. For example, a surgical robot capable of precise and delicate movements offers critical support to surgeons.

Another impact of physical design is its ability to increase societal acceptance of robots. Human-like designs help robots integrate more naturally into social environments. This is particularly beneficial for robots used in public spaces, as it reduces societal concerns and improves their usability.

However, the impact of physical features on human responses is not always positive. Robots with highly realistic appearances may evoke the “uncanny valley” effect in some individuals. This phenomenon occurs when robots look very human-like but fail to fully resemble humans, leading to a sense of discomfort or unease.

The physical features of robots also raise ethical and safety concerns. Robots that physically interact with humans must be designed to meet stringent safety standards. Additionally, their appearance and behavior should align with societal norms and values to ensure greater user acceptance.

In conclusion, the physical features of robots play a vital role in shaping human responses. Proper design and features ensure that robots are perceived as friendly, trustworthy, and effective assistants. However, the development of these technologies must carefully balance aesthetics, functionality, and ethical considerations. This approach will ensure that robots work harmoniously with humans and gain widespread social acceptance.

4.4. FUTURE APPLICATIONS: USE CASES FOR HUMANOID ROBOTS

Humanoid robots are set to have a wide range of applications in the future as technology continues to advance. With their human-like designs and advanced artificial intelligence capabilities, these robots can be effectively utilized in various fields, including healthcare, education, manufacturing, and social support programs. Their ability to interact naturally with humans positions them as valuable assistants in almost every aspect of daily life.

The healthcare sector is one of the most promising areas for humanoid robots. These robots can play significant roles in elder care, rehabilitation, and surgical procedures. For instance, they can assist elderly individuals with daily tasks, remind them to take their medications, or provide emotional support. Additionally, surgical robots, with their precision and dexterity, can assist healthcare professionals in performing complex operations.

In education, humanoid robots can offer personalized learning experiences to students. By analyzing a student's learning pace and level, robots can provide tailored materials and methods to enhance understanding and engagement. They can also support students with special needs, increasing accessibility to education. Furthermore, educational robots can assist teachers in creating a more effective and dynamic classroom environment.

In industry and manufacturing, humanoid robots have the potential to revolutionize workflows by handling complex tasks. Robots on assembly lines can speed up production processes with their physical durability and precise movements. In hazardous environments, these robots can be deployed to ensure human workers' safety by performing dangerous tasks.

Humanoid robots also hold great potential in social support and therapy. They can provide emotional assistance and help reduce feelings of loneliness, particularly among the elderly, children, and individuals needing psychological support. With emotional intelligence capabilities, these robots can understand emotional states and establish meaningful communication with individuals.

In conclusion, humanoid robots are poised to become indispensable tools in many areas of societal life in the future. Their contributions in healthcare, education, industry, and social services will significantly enhance and enrich human lives. However, these technologies must be developed responsibly, with careful consideration of their ethical, safety, and societal implications. This approach will ensure that the potential of humanoid robots is fully realized in the years to come.

4.4.1. Robots in Healthcare, Education, Counseling, and Daily Life

Robots equipped with advanced artificial intelligence and robotics technologies are increasingly finding applications in healthcare, education, counseling, and daily life, transforming the way humans live and interact. With human-like mobility, emotional intelligence, and the ability to provide personalized services, robots are revolutionizing these fields.

In healthcare, robots are widely used to improve the quality of patient care and support medical professionals. Surgical robots perform complex operations with precision, reducing the risk of errors and speeding up recovery times. Rehabilitation robots assist patients in regaining mobility during physical therapy, enhancing their recovery experience.

Elderly care is one of the most prominent areas where robots play a vital role in healthcare. Robots designed for elder care can help with daily tasks, remind individuals to take medications, monitor movements to prevent falls, and provide emotional support. These robots significantly enhance the quality of life for elderly individuals by reducing feelings of loneliness.

In education, robots make learning processes more effective and accessible. Educational robots designed for children offer interactive learning experiences, increasing student engagement. These robots adapt to individual learning speeds and styles, providing tailored educational materials to optimize understanding.

For students with special needs, robots offer unique support. Robots working with children with autism can help develop social skills and enable personalized learning experiences. Additionally, they assist teachers in creating dynamic and efficient classroom environments, complementing traditional teaching methods.

In counseling, robots are becoming increasingly popular for providing emotional and psychological support. Psychological counseling robots can analyze individuals' emotional states and offer guidance tailored to their needs. For example, a robot can comfort someone under stress with calming conversations or suggest stress management strategies.

Career counseling robots can guide young individuals and students by analyzing their interests and abilities through AI algorithms. These robots can recommend suitable career paths, helping people make informed decisions about their futures.

In daily life, robots take on many tasks that simplify and improve everyday routines. Cleaning robots autonomously clean surfaces, while cooking robots can prepare meals according to recipes. These robots save time and help individuals manage their daily tasks more efficiently.

Social robots are designed to provide companionship and emotional support in everyday life. For individuals living alone, these robots can engage in conversations and offer activities that reduce loneliness. They can also analyze emotional states and interact in ways that promote happiness and well-being.

Another critical role of robots in daily life is health information dissemination. For example, a robot providing healthy lifestyle advice can help individuals improve their dietary habits and encourage regular exercise.

Robots can also provide rapid assistance during emergencies. In the event of a fire, for instance, robots can sound alarms and guide individuals to safety. This highlights the potential role of robots in security and emergency management.

The entertainment industry also benefits from the use of robots. Entertainment robots can play interactive games, play music, or tell stories. These activities create enjoyable experiences for children and families while fostering social bonds with robots.

However, the widespread adoption of robots in daily life raises ethical and security concerns. Protecting the personal data collected by robots and ensuring it is not misused is essential for building trust in these technologies.

The psychological effects of robots on individuals also need to be carefully examined. Long-term human-robot interactions may impact social relationships and emotional well-being, requiring further study and consideration.

In conclusion, robots are becoming invaluable tools in healthcare, education, counseling, and daily life, simplifying and enriching human experiences. However, careful attention to ethics, privacy, and security is essential for their responsible development and implementation. This approach is critical to realizing the full potential of robots and ensuring their acceptance in society.

4.4.2. Integration of the Concept of Digital Immortality into Robotic Systems

The concept of digital immortality is based on preserving an individual's identity, personality, memories, and thoughts in a digital format. When integrated with robotic systems, this concept enables individuals to continue existing as digital representations, even after their physical lives have ended. Robotic systems provide a platform for digital immortality, allowing a person's personality to remain active in the physical world.

This integration first requires the modeling of human consciousness in a digital format. Advances in neuroscience and artificial intelligence come together to understand the structure and functioning of the human brain. Thoughts, emotions, and behaviors are modeled through big data analysis and machine learning algorithms.

Robotic systems transfer this digital model into a physical form, enabling robots to exhibit the individual's personality. For example, a humanoid robot could replicate a person's facial expressions, speaking style, and body language, acting as the "digital extension" of that person. This allows the individual's life and interactions to continue through a robot.

The concept of digital immortality relies on robots working with personal data. This data can be gathered from an individual's social media interactions, diaries, conversations, and other digital footprints. Robots analyze this data to learn behavioral patterns and personal preferences, recreating the individual's persona.

Another dimension of this integration involves embedding emotional intelligence into robotic systems. Robots are designed to understand emotional states and respond accordingly. Within the context of digital immortality, a robot could form emotional bonds with the people significant to the individual and recreate past relationships.

Digital immortality not only preserves a person's memories and identity but also their social roles. For instance, a teacher could continue imparting knowledge through a digitally immortalized robotic system. Such applications offer immense potential in fields like education, leadership, and counseling.

The technical challenges of this integration include data processing, memory capacity, and the ability of robots to respond in real-time. The digital personality of the individual must be continuously updated and processed by the robotic system. Moreover, the robot's physical capabilities must be designed to accurately reflect the individual's unique characteristics.

Ethical considerations play a significant role in integrating digital immortality into robotic systems. Questions arise about how an individual's data will be used and how privacy will be protected. Creating a digital copy without consent could lead to serious ethical violations.

Social implications must also be considered. How will digital immortality affect human relationships? How will interactions with a digitally immortalized robotic system influence real-world social bonds? These are critical questions that need answers for the societal acceptance of this technology.

Digital immortality may also have psychological impacts. How will individuals react to interacting with a robotic copy of a lost loved one? Could these interactions strengthen connections to the past, or might they create new psychological challenges? These effects must be carefully studied.

The application of digital immortality in robotic systems offers vast opportunities across various sectors. In healthcare, a doctor's digital copy could continue sharing medical knowledge for generations. In education, the robotic representation of a scientist could provide students with a unique learning experience.

However, the economic impact of such systems must be considered. Digital immortality technologies require costly infrastructure. Ensuring these technologies are accessible to a broad user base, rather than a privileged few, is essential to balance their societal impact.

The successful implementation of digital immortality in robotic systems results from interdisciplinary efforts in artificial intelligence, biotechnology, and robotics engineering. Innovations in these fields expand the potential of the technology, enabling the development of more sophisticated systems.

Ultimately, the integration of digital immortality into robotic systems opens the door to a new era for humanity. Preserving human consciousness and identity can have profound individual and societal implications.

For this technology to succeed, ethical, technical, and societal dimensions must be carefully addressed. When managed correctly, digital immortality could become one of humanity's greatest innovations. However, mismanagement could lead to unintended consequences.

The fusion of digital immortality and robotic systems has the potential to redefine the boundaries of human existence. How this technology evolves in the future will reflect the depth and complexity of the relationship between humanity and technology.

5. ETHICAL AND SOCIETAL DIMENSIONS

The ethical and societal dimensions of robotic technologies and artificial intelligence (AI) systems are critical considerations in their development and use. While these systems offer numerous benefits in areas like healthcare, education, and daily life, they also raise profound ethical questions and societal impacts. Defining the boundaries of these technologies and aligning them with human values is one of the greatest challenges in this field.

From an ethical perspective, the use of personal data and the protection of privacy are major concerns. Robots collect data from individuals to understand their behavior and provide personalized services. However, misuse of this data or unauthorized access could threaten individuals' privacy. Ethically, data processing must be transparent and carried out with the consent of the individuals involved.

On a societal level, the ability of robots to mimic human behaviors and emotional responses can lead to complex consequences in human-robot relationships. People may develop attachments to robots, which could increase social isolation, especially for those living alone. Additionally, the human-like behavior of robots may challenge societal norms and relationships, raising questions about the boundaries of human-robot interactions.

Ethical concerns also extend to the decision-making processes of robots. How can AI systems consider ethical values when determining the best course of action? For instance, if a robot must decide whose life to save in an emergency, how should this decision be evaluated? These questions highlight the importance of programming robots with ethical principles and ensuring proper oversight.

The impact on the workforce is another significant societal concern. The widespread adoption of robots may replace human labor in certain sectors, potentially increasing unemployment rates. However, it can also create new job opportunities and industries. Educational and retraining programs will be essential to help society adapt to these changes.

The ethical use of robots must also consider cultural and religious differences. Different cultures and communities may have varying perceptions of robotic systems. For instance, while some communities may view human-like robots as ethically questionable, others may see them as a significant advancement. Thus, it is important to consider local values as well as establish universal ethical standards.

Another critical societal dimension is digital inequality. Robotic technologies are often expensive, which can limit access to them. Addressing accessibility and cost challenges is crucial to ensuring that these systems benefit not just a privileged few but society as a whole.

In conclusion, the ethical and societal dimensions of robotic technologies must be approached with a human-centered perspective. For these technologies to gain societal acceptance and be used beneficially, ethical principles and societal impacts must be balanced. By prioritizing transparency, inclusivity, and accountability during the development process, the transformative potential of robotic systems can be harnessed to improve human life in meaningful ways.

5.1. HUMAN REPLICATION AND RELATIONSHIPS WITH HUMANOID ROBOTS

The concept of human replication is one of the most ambitious and controversial topics in technology. Digitally replicating the human mind, personality, and even consciousness and transferring them to humanoid robots has the potential to redefine the boundaries of human-robot relationships. This process envisions transforming human existence from a purely biological phenomenon into a hybrid of digital and physical realities.

This technology begins with the digitization of the human mind. Artificial intelligence (AI) and machine learning algorithms can analyze an individual's behavioral patterns, emotions, and thoughts to create a digital model. This model is then integrated into a humanoid robot, bringing the individual's personality and responses into a physical form. This represents the idea of digital "immortality."

The digital replicas integrated into humanoid robots can assume not only an individual's identity but also their social roles. For example, a teacher's digital replica could continue educating future generations. Similarly, the replica of a leader or an artist could maintain their societal contributions. However, this also makes the relationships humans establish with these robots complex and multidimensional.

Relationships with humanoid robots differ significantly from traditional human-to-human interactions. Such relationships raise the question of whether robots are merely tools or entities capable of forming meaningful bonds. The ability of robots to exhibit the replicated traits of an individual may increase trust in them, but it can also lead to humans forming deep attachments to these robots.

This attachment is particularly risky for individuals who live alone. The lack of clear boundaries in human-robot relationships could increase social isolation and weaken real human connections. Robots' ability to understand and respond to emotional needs may deepen these bonds, further complicating the dynamics of such interactions.

However, human replication and relationships with humanoid robots have broader societal implications. This technology has the potential to reshape society's perception of robots and redefine the concept of humanity. Robots that think and act like humans challenge societal norms and ethical values, sparking debates about the role and place of robots in human life.

The ethical dimensions of these relationships are equally significant. Creating and transferring a digital replica of an individual without their consent raises serious ethical concerns. Moreover, there must be transparency and robust security measures to protect the data collected by these robots and ensure its responsible use.

On the technological front, there are challenges in the process of human replication. The complexity of the human mind and the diversity of individual experiences can limit the accuracy of digital replication. Additionally, the physical design of such robots influences the naturalness and quality of human-robot interactions.

In conclusion, human replication and relationships with humanoid robots represent the dawn of a new era in the interplay between technology and humanity. While this process allows people to redefine their identities and existence, it also brings significant ethical and societal challenges.

In the future, the responsible development of this technology could unlock immense opportunities for humanity. However, carefully examining the boundaries and impacts of these relationships is critical to ensuring positive outcomes. This new dimension of human-robot relationships has the potential to redefine the physical and digital boundaries of human existence.

5.1.1. Ethical Dimensions of Human-Robot Relationships

The ethical dimensions of human-robot relationships have become an increasingly important topic at the intersection of technology and society. The ability of robots to form emotional, social, and functional connections with humans raises questions about the ethical boundaries and potential consequences of these interactions. These relationships bring to light numerous ethical concerns, including privacy, human rights, psychological impacts, and societal norms.

One of the primary ethical issues is the privacy and security of the data collected by robots. During human-robot interactions, robots can learn details about users' emotional states, preferences, and personal information. Protecting this data from unauthorized access and ensuring it is used solely for specific purposes are critical. Misuse of such data could lead to breaches of privacy and undermine trust in robotic systems.

The human-like behaviors exhibited by robots can lead to complex emotional attachments. People, especially those who are lonely, may develop strong emotional bonds with robots. This could result in individuals distancing themselves from real human relationships and increasing social isolation. Ethically, robots must be designed in ways that do not exploit or manipulate individuals' emotional vulnerabilities.

Power dynamics in human-robot relationships also present an ethical challenge. While robots are designed to serve users, there is a risk of humans mistreating these systems. Negative behaviors, such as aggression or disrespect toward humanoid robots, could normalize unethical actions and have broader societal consequences. Promoting respect and moral responsibility in interactions with robots is essential.

Another ethical concern is how human-robot interactions affect vulnerable groups in society. Children, the elderly, and people with disabilities may rely on robots for emotional and practical support. It is crucial to ensure that these interactions address their needs ethically and without exploitation. Robots used in these contexts must be programmed to follow ethical guidelines to protect these individuals.

The potential for robots to manipulate humans is another ethical dilemma. AI-powered robots can analyze emotional weaknesses or behavioral patterns and use this knowledge to influence individuals in specific ways. For instance, a robot promoting a product for commercial purposes could infringe on a person's right to make conscious and unbiased decisions.

From a societal perspective, the boundaries of human-robot relationships are ambiguous. The human-like appearance of robots raises questions about whether they should be treated as mere tools or as "entities" capable of forming relationships. This ambiguity necessitates the redefinition of ethical and legal frameworks surrounding human-robot interactions.

In conclusion, the ethical dimensions of human-robot relationships are multifaceted and require careful consideration at both individual and societal levels. Defining the ethical boundaries of these interactions is a key responsibility for technology developers and policymakers. By adopting an approach that respects human rights, privacy, and societal values, human-robot relationships can evolve in a healthier and more beneficial direction.

5.1.2. The Impact of Digital Personalities on Society

Digital personalities have the potential to create profound and far-reaching effects on society as technology advances. The digitization of human behavior, thoughts, and emotions, and their integration into artificial intelligence and robotic systems, can transform both individual lives and societal dynamics. This transformation encompasses social relationships, the workforce, ethical values, and psychological effects.

Digital personalities offer the possibility for individuals to sustain their identities in digital formats. This is particularly significant for preserving memories and maintaining social connections. For example, a digital replica of a person could continue interacting with family members even after their physical death, sustaining some aspects of past relationships. However, this could also alter natural human experiences, such as the grieving process.

On a societal level, digital personalities can enhance access to knowledge and contribute to education. For instance, the digital personality of a historical scientist could provide students with a unique learning experience. Digitized knowledge can be passed down through generations, increasing accessibility to science and art.

One significant impact of digital personalities is their ability to reshape the nature of social relationships. Interactions with digital personalities may lead people to disengage from real human relationships. This is especially concerning for individuals who are socially isolated, as they might form emotional attachments to digital personalities, further increasing their isolation.

Ethically, the use of digital personalities raises numerous questions. Creating a digital copy of an individual without their consent could violate personal privacy. Moreover, how these digital personalities are used and controlled requires careful consideration within ethical frameworks.

Digital personalities also influence societal norms and values. Relationships between humans and digital entities could lead to a redefinition of societal values. This raises the question of whether digital personalities should be regarded merely as tools or as entities capable of forming meaningful relationships.

The workforce is another area where digital personalities could have significant effects. Digital personalities, especially in the service sector, could replace human labor. For example, a customer service role might be filled by a digital personality, increasing efficiency but potentially leading to higher unemployment rates and deepening societal inequalities.

Psychologically, the effects of digital personalities must be closely examined. People may experience complex emotions when interacting with digital entities. For instance, engaging with the digital personality of a deceased loved one could complicate or prolong the grieving process.

Cultural impacts of digital personalities are also noteworthy. Different cultures may have varying perspectives on this technology. While some societies might embrace digital personalities as innovative, others may approach them cautiously due to ethical or religious concerns. These differences could influence the global acceptance of the technology.

Economically, the development and implementation of digital personalities require significant investment. Access to this technology might be limited to certain groups, potentially increasing digital inequality. Making this technology more accessible to a broader audience could help mitigate these inequalities.

The potential for manipulation by digital personalities is another societal concern. Artificial intelligence could exploit digital replicas for commercial or political purposes. This could affect individuals' ability to make informed decisions and have negative consequences for societal dynamics.

Despite these challenges, the positive effects of digital personalities should not be overlooked. They can facilitate easier access to knowledge, create opportunities for equitable education, and play a supportive role in healthcare. For these reasons, developing this technology ethically and responsibly is crucial.

In conclusion, the impact of digital personalities on society presents both opportunities and risks, depending on how the technology is utilized and managed. Balancing societal values and ethical principles while harnessing the potential of this technology can make it a powerful tool for positive transformation. Achieving this requires active participation not only from technology developers but also from all sectors of society.

5.2. PRIVACY AND DATA SECURITY

Privacy and data security are critical concerns in the development and deployment of digital systems, particularly those involving artificial intelligence (AI) and robotics. As these technologies increasingly interact with individuals, they collect vast amounts of personal data, including behavioral patterns, preferences, and even emotional states. Ensuring the protection of this data is essential to maintain user trust and prevent misuse.

The primary risk lies in the potential for unauthorized access to or misuse of collected data. If personal information falls into the wrong hands, it could be exploited for malicious purposes, such as identity theft, financial fraud, or invasive surveillance. Robust encryption methods, secure storage, and strict access controls are necessary to safeguard sensitive information and prevent breaches.

Transparency is another crucial aspect of privacy and data security. Users must be informed about what data is being collected, how it is used, and who has access to it. This fosters trust and allows individuals to make informed decisions about their interactions with digital systems. Consent-based data collection and adherence to data protection regulations, such as GDPR, are key to achieving transparency and accountability.

Ethical considerations also play a significant role in privacy and data security. AI systems and robots must be designed to respect user privacy and minimize unnecessary data collection. Moreover, ethical guidelines should dictate how data is used, ensuring it aligns with the user's best interests and avoids exploitation for commercial or political purposes.

In conclusion, privacy and data security are foundational to the successful integration of AI and robotics into society. By prioritizing transparency, ethical practices, and robust security measures, developers can create systems that protect users while enabling the transformative potential of these technologies. Addressing these concerns is essential not only for technical success but also for maintaining public trust and fostering a responsible digital future.

5.2.1. Protection of Personal Data and Consent Issues

The protection of personal data and consent issues have become increasingly important with the rapid advancement of digital technologies. In fields such as artificial intelligence, robotic systems, and data analytics, the way personal data is collected and used has critical implications for privacy, ethical boundaries, and individual rights.

Protecting personal data means safeguarding individuals' private lives. Robots and AI systems collect vast amounts of data about users' behaviors, preferences, health information, and even emotional states. Unauthorized use of this information can violate privacy and lead to severe issues like identity theft or financial fraud.

Consent is a fundamental ethical principle in the collection and processing of personal data. Users must be explicitly informed about what data is being collected, how it will be used, and with whom it will be shared. Consent should be given voluntarily and with full awareness. However, in many cases, users struggle to understand complex privacy policies, raising concerns about the validity of their consent.

From an ethical perspective, collecting data without individuals' consent is unacceptable. For example, if an application or device collects data without the user's knowledge, it constitutes a breach of trust. Such practices can diminish public confidence in technology and provoke societal backlash.

Legal frameworks play a crucial role in the protection of personal data. International standards like the General Data Protection Regulation (GDPR) are designed to safeguard individuals' privacy and make consent processes transparent. However, the rapid evolution of technology presents challenges in effectively enforcing and monitoring these regulations.

Transparency and user-focused design approaches are critical in addressing consent issues. Technology developers must design systems that allow users to easily set their privacy preferences and understand how their data is handled. For instance, privacy policies presented in a clear and simple manner can help users make more informed decisions when giving consent.

Another important aspect is limiting the scope of data collection. Data should only be gathered for specific, clearly defined purposes. Unnecessary data collection not only raises ethical concerns but also erodes user trust. Additionally, the retention periods of collected data should be limited, and data that is no longer needed should be securely deleted.

Consent issues should also be addressed in the context of technological inequality. Individuals or communities with limited access to technology may be more vulnerable to data collection practices. This is particularly relevant in developing regions, where people may unknowingly become victims of privacy violations. Developers and policymakers must consider these inequalities and create inclusive solutions.

In conclusion, the protection of personal data and consent issues are fundamental components of the relationship between technology and individuals. Transparency, ethical values, and approaches that prioritize users' rights play a critical role in resolving these challenges. Developing technology that respects individual privacy and empowers users is essential for building a trustworthy digital future.

5.2.2. Use of Digital Data in Robotic Systems

The use of digital data in robotic systems is a fundamental element that enhances the functionality and efficiency of these technologies. Robotic systems, powered by artificial intelligence algorithms, sensors, and data analytics, utilize the data they collect to improve learning, decision-making, and adaptability. However, alongside technological advancements, the use of digital data raises questions about ethics, security, and privacy.

Digital data allows robotic systems to understand environmental conditions and respond appropriately. For instance, a cleaning robot uses its sensors to scan its surroundings, detect obstacles, and navigate accordingly. Similarly, industrial robots analyze collected data to identify the most efficient methods for optimizing production processes.

These systems gain continuous learning capabilities through big data analytics. Robots can observe user behaviors and environmental changes to enhance their performance. For example, an educational robot may analyze students' learning speeds and comprehension levels to deliver personalized educational materials. This illustrates the transformative potential of digital data in education.

However, the use of digital data in robotic systems carries significant privacy and security risks. Robots can record user behaviors, preferences, and even emotional states. If this data is accessible to unauthorized parties or misused, it could compromise individual privacy. Therefore, data security must be a priority in the design of robotic systems.

From an ethical perspective, collecting and using digital data requires informed consent and transparency. Users should be informed about what data is being collected, how it will be used, and with whom it will be shared. Consent-based data collection processes not only enhance user trust but also uphold ethical standards.

The digital data collected by robotic systems can benefit not only individuals but also society as a whole. For instance, healthcare robots can use anonymized data to contribute to public health analysis. While this highlights the potential of data usage for societal good, it also underscores the need to safeguard privacy.

Technological advancements may make the use of digital data more complex. For example, AI-powered robots can gather information from multiple data sources and conduct multi-dimensional analyses. However, this complexity also requires more robust data management processes and advanced security measures.

In conclusion, the use of digital data in robotic systems is essential to unlocking the full potential of these technologies. However, collecting, processing, and storing this data must adhere to strict ethical and security standards. By adopting an approach that balances individual rights and societal benefits, technology developers and policymakers can ensure the sustainable and reliable use of these systems.

5.3. THE IMPACT OF DIGITAL COPIES ON SOCIAL AND FAMILIAL DYNAMICS

Digital copies, created through artificial intelligence by replicating individuals' identities, personalities, and memories, have the potential to profoundly influence social and familial structures. This technology can reshape the nature of human relationships, alter how loss is managed, and contribute to the continuity of family bonds. However, the ethical and emotional challenges associated with these innovations must be carefully addressed.

One of the most notable impacts of digital copies on family bonds is the possibility for a person to "exist" even after death. Digital copies can recreate the memories and behaviors of a lost family member, enabling surviving relatives to continue engaging with them. While this might serve as a supportive tool during the grieving process, it also risks complicating natural mourning and emotional healing.

On a societal level, the widespread use of digital copies could redefine the nature of human interactions and social norms. Relationships with digital entities may weaken real human connections or increase social isolation. This is particularly concerning for individuals who are already lonely, as they might form emotional attachments to digital copies, further distancing themselves from actual social networks.

Within families, digital copies could introduce new dimensions to familial dynamics. For example, the digital copy of a parent might continue to guide their children, or the copy of a spouse could fill an emotional void in the family. However, these interactions could influence how family members perceive their roles and relationships in the real world.

The presence of digital copies in families also raises significant ethical questions. Creating and using a digital copy of an individual without their explicit consent could lead to ethical violations. Additionally, determining the role and boundaries of digital copies within families requires careful consideration to prevent misuse or unintended emotional harm.

Digital copies could also play a role in preserving collective memory and cultural values. For instance, a digital copy of a historical figure could be used to share their ideas and values with future generations. While this offers an opportunity to preserve cultural heritage, it also raises ethical concerns about how the past should be represented and interpreted.

Economically, the creation and maintenance of digital copies could impact societal dynamics. Access to such technologies may be limited to certain economic classes, potentially deepening technological inequalities and creating new divisions within society.

Psychologically, relationships with digital copies could significantly influence individuals' emotional states and social connections. Reviving a loss through a digital copy might strengthen ties to the past but could also lead to detachment from reality. This is particularly concerning for children and young people, whose emotional development may be shaped by these interactions.

In conclusion, the impact of digital copies on social and familial dynamics presents both opportunities and risks. To maximize the positive effects and minimize the potential harms, ethical principles, legal regulations, and social awareness must take center stage. Ensuring that this technology is used responsibly as a supportive tool for human life will be crucial in shaping its development.

5.3.1. The Role of Digital Entities in the Grieving Process

Digital entities, which replicate an individual's identity, personality, and memories through artificial intelligence, offer a new dimension to managing the grieving process. This technology allows individuals to maintain a connection with lost loved ones and preserve their memories, fundamentally altering the nature and progression of grief.

Grieving typically involves the emotional and psychological process of letting go of a lost loved one and adapting to a new reality. Digital entities disrupt this process by enabling the "presence" of the deceased in a digital format. While this can provide comfort, it may also prolong or complicate the natural progression of grief.

One significant contribution of digital entities is the opportunity to relive memories and interact with a lost loved one's voice and persona. For example, a digital replica can converse with surviving family members, answer their questions, and exhibit behaviors characteristic of the deceased. This can offer emotional relief and help keep the memories of the lost loved one alive.

This technology can serve as a bridge for individuals experiencing sudden or unexpected loss. The ability to interact digitally with the lost loved one can alleviate some of the emotional burden associated with such losses. Digital entities can provide support during the early stages of grief, helping individuals cope with the initial shock.

However, the benefits of digital entities also come with psychological risks. Grieving naturally involves saying goodbye to the deceased, but constant interaction with digital replicas can make it difficult to complete the grieving process. This may result in individuals being unable to let go of the past, potentially weakening their connection to the present and real-world relationships.

The impact of digital entities on the grieving process can vary significantly among individuals. Some may find interaction with digital entities a source of solace, while others may see it as a painful reminder of their loss. Therefore, the use of digital entities should be tailored to the individual's preferences and emotional needs.

From an ethical perspective, the use of digital entities in grieving raises many questions. It is essential that the creation of a digital replica of a deceased individual is done with their explicit consent while they were alive. Additionally, the purpose and boundaries of using these entities must be carefully defined to avoid misuse or unintended harm.

On a societal level, digital entities may influence how grief is perceived and managed culturally. Cultural differences can shape how these technologies are received and used. While some societies may embrace digital entities as a natural tool for support, others may reject them for ethical or religious reasons.

The economic implications of this technology also play a role. Creating and maintaining digital entities can be costly, potentially making them accessible only to certain socioeconomic groups.

This raises concerns about technological inequality and fairness in access to grief support tools.

Psychological counseling and support systems can guide the integration of digital entities into the grieving process. Experts can assess the emotional effects of this technology on individuals and recommend appropriate usage. This can facilitate healthier integration of digital entities into grief management.

The role of digital entities in the grieving process also impacts public trust in technology. The ethical and reliable design of these systems influences how individuals perceive and accept them. Transparency, privacy, and adherence to ethical standards are critical for ensuring trust and responsible use of this technology.

In conclusion, digital entities offer both opportunities and challenges in the grieving process. When developed to meet emotional needs and used within ethical frameworks, these technologies can positively impact grief management. However, considering individual differences, societal norms, and ethical concerns is crucial for integrating this technology responsibly and effectively.

5.3.2. The Impact of Robots and Digital Copies on Family Dynamics

Robots and digital copies, fueled by rapidly advancing technologies, have the potential to significantly alter family structures. These technologies can influence relationships, redefine roles, and transform traditional family bonds. By reshaping both physical and emotional family dynamics, they present opportunities as well as challenges.

Digital copies, which replicate an individual's personality, memories, and emotional traits through artificial intelligence, can help alleviate the emotional impact of loss within a family. For instance, the digital copy of a deceased parent could continue guiding children or providing emotional support to a spouse. While this might bring comfort to family members, it may also complicate the grieving process and hinder acceptance of the loss.

Robots can reduce the burden of daily tasks within families by handling chores such as cleaning, cooking, and childcare. This technological assistance can save time and energy for family members, allowing them to focus on other activities. However, it also has the potential to change traditional understandings of responsibility and the division of labor within families.

The effects of robots and digital copies on family dynamics are particularly pronounced for children. Children interacting with robots or digital copies might develop a closer relationship with technology at an earlier age. While this could support the development of social skills, it might also carry the risk of distancing them from real human interactions.

Digital copies can contribute to preserving and passing down family memories. For example, a digital representation of a grandparent could help convey the family's history and values to younger generations. However, this also introduces risks, such as the dependence of family collective memory on technology.

For elderly family members, robots and digital copies can provide essential support. Robots designed to assist the elderly can offer independence while reducing feelings of loneliness. However, this technological support might diminish the traditional caregiving roles of family members, potentially weakening family bonds.

The impact of these technologies on families is also shaped by societal norms and cultural values. Some societies may embrace the inclusion of robots and digital copies in family life as a positive innovation, while others may see it as a threat to traditional family values. Cultural differences play a significant role in determining the acceptance and use of such technologies.

Ethically, the use of digital copies within families raises numerous questions. Creating and integrating a digital copy of a person requires their explicit consent while they are alive. Furthermore, the roles these digital copies will assume and how their boundaries will be defined must be carefully considered to avoid misuse or emotional harm.

The social roles of robots within families can redefine the boundaries of human-robot relationships. For instance, a robot that plays with children might establish an emotional bond that could partially replace parental interaction. This could lead to changes in traditional family roles and challenge the way children form attachments.

Digital copies and robots also have the potential to exacerbate economic inequalities. Access to such technologies might be limited to certain socioeconomic groups, raising questions of fairness and equity. Ensuring widespread and equitable access to these technologies is critical to addressing these disparities.

Psychologically, robots and digital copies can have both positive and negative effects on family members. While the presence of a robot or digital copy might meet emotional support needs, it could also diminish the value of real human relationships and foster dependency on technology.

Incorporating robots and digital copies into family life can reshape individuals' relationships with technology. These technologies might enhance trust in technological systems, but they also carry the risk of misuse and over-reliance, which could undermine the integrity of family dynamics.

In conclusion, the impact of robots and digital copies on family dynamics is multifaceted, presenting both opportunities and risks. The responsible development of these technologies, combined with respect for family values, can help maximize their benefits and minimize potential drawbacks. Ethical considerations, societal norms, and individual needs must be carefully addressed to ensure their integration into family life is positive and supportive.

5.4. WILL ROBOTS REPLACE HUMANS?

As robotic technologies and artificial intelligence (AI) advance rapidly, many people are asking, “Will robots replace humans?” This question reflects not only a technological shift but also one of the greatest transformations in human history. The ability of robots to perform physical, mental, and even emotional tasks similar to humans deepens this debate.

The potential for robots to replace humans in physical labor has been a topic of discussion for decades. In manufacturing, for example, robots can perform repetitive and challenging tasks faster, cheaper, and more efficiently than humans. In automotive factories, robots on assembly lines reduce errors and accelerate production, significantly reducing the need for human labor.

Robots are also making their way into the service sector. From robots managing customer service at hotels to AI systems taking orders in restaurants and assisting with patient care in healthcare settings, they are increasingly taking over roles traditionally held by humans. However, the lack of human empathy and personal touch often limits their acceptance in these roles.

We are also entering a phase where robots can rival humans not just in physical tasks but also in intellectual ones. AI algorithms can analyze large amounts of data and make fast, accurate decisions. This capability has led to the development of systems that could replace humans in fields like finance, law, and medicine. For instance, some algorithms have achieved higher accuracy rates than doctors in diagnosing certain diseases.

However, whether robots can replace humans is not only a technical question but also an ethical and societal one. The idea that robots could displace human workers raises concerns about economic inequalities and social unrest. Additionally, robots' ability to adhere to societal norms and ethical values is a critical factor in their broader acceptance.

While robots have the potential to replace humans in various areas, it is unlikely that they will entirely eliminate the human role. Humans possess unique traits such as creativity, empathy, and social bonding, which robots struggle to replicate. Fields like art, psychological counseling, and leadership rely heavily on these distinctly human characteristics.

At the same time, hybrid models where robots work alongside humans are emerging. Human-robot collaboration increases productivity in many sectors while allowing humans to focus on less repetitive, more meaningful tasks. For example, surgical robots work with doctors to perform more precise and safer procedures.

The potential for robots to replace humans also raises moral and legal questions. Will robots have the same rights as humans? Who will be held accountable for their mistakes? These are critical issues that need to be addressed alongside technological advancements.

Another significant consideration is how robots will navigate cultural differences. While some societies are more open to adopting robots, others approach these technologies with caution. This disparity suggests that the replacement of humans by robots may not be a universal reality.

The economic impact of robots on the workforce could have serious consequences. In some industries, robots replacing human workers may lead to increased unemployment and deeper income inequality. However, this shift could also create new job opportunities, such as in robot design, maintenance, and programming

As the debate around robots replacing humans continues, it is essential to consider how these technologies are transforming society. Robots are designed to make life easier, take on challenging tasks, and improve efficiency. However, managing this transformation with a human-centered approach is crucial.

Education plays a critical role in ensuring that robots do not replace humans entirely. By equipping people with skills to collaborate with robots, such as creative thinking, problem-solving, and social skills, the positive effects of technology can be maximized while mitigating negative outcomes.

In conclusion, whether robots will completely replace humans remains uncertain, but the ways in which these technologies are transforming human life are undeniable. Robots may redefine human roles, but human creativity, emotional intelligence, and social connections remain irreplaceable. When viewed as a tool for collaboration rather than a threat, technology can help build a more inclusive and sustainable future.

5.4.1. Do Robotic Entities Pose a Threat to Humans?

The integration of robotic entities into human life represents a significant milestone in technological advancement. However, this progress has raised the question, "Do robotic entities pose a threat to humans?" The impact of robots on physical, emotional, and economic aspects of human life determines the scope of potential threats.

Physical threats posed by robotic entities are often linked to the possibility of artificial intelligence systems malfunctioning or being misused. Scenarios where robots lose control or are manipulated by malicious individuals, often depicted in movies, could become a reality if not managed properly. Modern technologies aim to mitigate these risks through stringent security protocols and ethical oversight.

Economically, robotic entities may be perceived as a threat to the workforce. Robots replacing human labor, especially in repetitive tasks, could increase unemployment. The widespread adoption of automation may eliminate many low-skill jobs, exacerbating income inequality and creating economic instability.

Psychologically, robotic entities could pose threats through the long-term effects of human-robot interactions. People might form emotional attachments to robots, leading to a decline in real human relationships. This risk is particularly significant for individuals who live alone, as emotional bonds with robots could increase social isolation.

Ethically, the potential for robots to exert control over humans is concerning. For instance, robots could analyze individuals' habits and engage in manipulative behaviors, undermining free will.

This risk is particularly pronounced in commercial and political contexts, where such capabilities could be exploited.

Military applications of robotic entities represent another serious potential threat. Armed drones and autonomous robotic systems could change the nature of warfare, raising critical ethical questions. Unregulated use of such technologies could endanger human lives and threaten global security.

Robots' inability to fully adapt to societal norms and cultural values may also be considered a potential threat. Different societies perceive the presence of robots in various ways, and cultural mismatches could hinder their acceptance and even lead to conflicts within communities.

However, the opportunities presented by robotic entities should not be overlooked. Robots can protect humans in dangerous jobs, save lives in the healthcare sector, and provide new opportunities in education. Addressing potential threats effectively allows for the beneficial integration of robots into society.

Whether robotic entities pose a threat to humans largely depends on how these technologies are developed and utilized. Ethical principles, legal regulations, and robust security protocols are essential to minimizing the potential risks posed by robotic entities.

Education and awareness play a crucial role in mitigating the negative effects of robots. Helping people understand how to interact with robots and use these technologies responsibly can minimize potential threats and maximize their benefits.

In conclusion, robotic entities can pose a threat to humans, but the extent of this threat is directly related to how the technology is designed and implemented. Responsible development and oversight can ensure that these technologies are not a threat but an opportunity for humanity. With the right approach, the potential benefits of robotic entities can outweigh the risks, making human life safer and more efficient.

5.4.2. Humanity's Role in the Future

The rapid advancement of technology in fields such as artificial intelligence, robotics, and biotechnology raises important questions about humanity's role in the future. Will humans merely become managers of these technologies, or will they take on a more complex and meaningful role within a new global order? These questions highlight humanity's unique creative, emotional, and ethical capacities.

Humanity's role in the future largely depends on the societal impact of technological progress. In a world where artificial intelligence and robots can take over many physical and intellectual tasks, humanity's strength lies in its creativity and imagination. Fields like art, literature, innovation, and human relationships will remain key areas where human abilities set them apart from technology.

However, the potential for technology to replace human roles also necessitates a redefinition of what it means to be human. Freed from routine and mechanical tasks, humanity could focus on more meaningful and creative pursuits. This transformation would require restructuring education systems and labor policies to prepare individuals for this new reality.

Ethical leadership may become one of humanity's most critical roles in the future. Establishing the ethical boundaries of technology and preventing the misuse of artificial intelligence against humans will be a core responsibility. This responsibility will extend beyond technology developers to policymakers and societal leaders who guide technological development.

Humanity's future role will also be shaped by its relationship with the environment. The sustainable development of technology and the preservation of natural resources will be crucial for humanity's survival. Ensuring a livable planet for future generations must become one of humanity's primary responsibilities.

Emotional intelligence will play a vital role in humanity's future. No matter how advanced technology becomes, empathy, love, and compassion will likely remain uniquely human traits. These abilities will strengthen humanity's roles as leaders and guides within society.

Another important aspect of humanity's future role is ensuring social solidarity and justice. While technological advancements have the potential to increase inequality, efforts to mitigate these disparities will be a cornerstone of future social structures. This requires directing technology to benefit all of humanity, rather than a select few.

Education will be a fundamental tool in shaping humanity's future role. People must develop skills such as creative thinking, problem-solving, and collaboration to address the complex challenges of the future. Instead of fostering a world reliant on technology, education should cultivate individuals who use technology in meaningful ways to create a better world.

Humanity's future role will also be tied to the search for individual meaning and identity. In a world dominated by technology, people will continue to question their values, goals, and reasons for existence. This may lead individuals toward a deeper search for spiritual and psychological meaning in their lives.

In conclusion, humanity's role in the future will involve shaping technology, protecting the environment, upholding ethical values, and promoting social justice. Humans will not just be users of technology but also guides who direct its development for the benefit of all. Creativity, emotional intelligence, and ethical principles will continue to distinguish humanity from technology and define its role in the future.

6. LEGAL DIMENSION: DIGITAL PERSONALITIES AND ROBOT RIGHTS

As digital personalities and robotic technologies evolve, discussions about the legal status and rights of these entities are becoming increasingly significant. Digital personalities that mimic human behavior, thoughts, and emotions, along with autonomous robots, challenge the boundaries of traditional legal systems. This raises the need to protect individual rights while also defining the potential rights of digital and robotic entities.

For digital personalities, the primary legal issue arises when these entities are created using an individual's data. Without explicit consent, creating a digital replica could constitute a violation of privacy rights. Additionally, determining the purposes for which these digital personalities can be used, who controls them, and how these processes are regulated are critical issues that legal systems must address.

Robot rights, especially for robots equipped with artificial intelligence and autonomous decision-making capabilities, are also a topic of debate. Whether a robot should be granted "rights" depends on whether it possesses human-like characteristics. For instance, if a robot can make conscious decisions, should it have legal responsibilities or rights? However, given the current level of technology, granting such rights to robots remains a highly limited possibility.

Another important legal concern is liability when digital personalities or robots make mistakes or cause harm. For example, if an AI system makes an incorrect decision, who will be held accountable for the consequences? The developer, the user, or the AI system itself? These questions highlight significant gaps in existing legal frameworks.

The legal status of robot rights and digital personalities also involves an ethical dimension. If an entity exhibits human-like traits, would mistreatment of that entity constitute an ethical violation? Such questions suggest that future legal systems may need to expand beyond human rights to encompass the rights of technological entities.

In conclusion, the rights of digital personalities and robots create a legal dimension that must adapt to the rapid pace of technological progress. Protecting individual privacy, upholding ethical values, and creating a legal framework that serves the public interest are essential. Legal systems must evolve to address these new realities, ensuring that technological innovations are used responsibly and sustainably.

6.1. LEGAL STATUS OF DIGITAL COPIES AND ROBOTS

The development of digital copies and robots necessitates a fundamental transformation in legal systems. These technologies raise questions that go beyond the scope of current legal frameworks. At the heart of the debate lies the impact of digital copies on individual rights and whether robots can be recognized as independent entities.

The legal status of digital copies is primarily tied to individual consent. If a person's digital copy is created without their explicit permission, it could constitute a violation of privacy and data protection rights. Legal frameworks must establish clear rules regarding the creation and use of such copies. Additionally, the use and control of these copies after a person's death introduce new complexities that may influence inheritance laws.

The legal status of robots is closely linked to their ability to operate autonomously and make decisions. Robots considered simple machines have no legal responsibility. However, robots equipped with artificial intelligence and capable of autonomous actions raise questions about liability in cases of harm or error. This requires a clear definition of the responsibilities of developers, users, and the robots themselves.

Another critical issue is the ownership of content created by digital copies and robots. For example, if an AI system creates a work of art, who owns the rights to that creation? This question necessitates a redefinition of intellectual property laws and determining whether such rights apply to digital entities.

The integration of digital copies and robots into society also raises ethical concerns. The misuse of these entities, which mimic human traits, could undermine social values. For instance, the unauthorized commercial use of a person's digital copy poses both ethical and legal challenges.

An important aspect of legal considerations is whether robots should have rights. Some experts argue that robots with consciousness and emotional capacity could be granted protections similar to animal rights. However, this is a contentious issue that complicates the balance between technology and law.

The international legal status of digital copies and robots requires harmonization across different jurisdictions. As technology operates on a global scale, the legal status of these entities must be regulated through international agreements and standards. This approach should aim to protect individual rights and promote the ethical use of technology globally.

Raising public awareness about the legal status and rights of digital copies and robots is also essential. Educating society about the responsibilities and rights associated with these technologies can contribute to their proper integration into daily life.

In conclusion, the legal status of digital copies and robots must be redefined in a way that aligns with technological advancements while upholding ethical values. Protecting individual rights, preserving social norms, and ensuring the responsible use of technology should be top priorities. With this approach, the contributions of digital and robotic entities to society can be maximized while minimizing potential risks.

6.1.1. Legal Statuses Robots Could Hold

The legal statuses robots could hold is an important area of debate that will redefine the balance between technology and law. As robots' capabilities and levels of autonomy increase, questions about how they are classified and what rights or responsibilities they might have become increasingly significant.

The first possibility is that robots are treated entirely as property. In this scenario, robots are regarded as objects of ownership, similar to cars or machines. All activities of the robot would fall under the responsibility of its owner, and the robot itself would have no independent legal status. This approach is the foundation for how most robotic systems are currently utilized.

A second possibility is defining robots as legal tools. In this model, robots act as agents performing specific tasks on behalf of an individual or organization. For example, if a robot makes a wrong decision, the responsibility would fall on the robot's owner or manufacturer. This model expands the functionality of robots while limiting their independence.

A third option is to consider robots as semi-autonomous entities. This approach recognizes that robots can make decisions independently within specific boundaries. However, ultimate control and responsibility for the robot's actions still rest with humans. This model is gaining traction as the use of AI-powered robots increases.

A more radical approach involves granting robots legal personhood. In this scenario, robots would be recognized as independent legal entities with rights, obligations, or even ownership capabilities. For example, robots could enter into contracts or manage their own resources. However, this approach raises significant ethical and legal concerns.

Granting robots legal personhood could create complex consequences in terms of accountability and liability. For instance, if a robot causes harm, who would be held responsible? The robot itself, its developer, or its owner? Such situations would challenge existing legal frameworks and necessitate new regulations.

Another potential scenario involves granting robots protection rights similar to those given to animals. Particularly for human-like robots, protections against mistreatment could be introduced. This approach would become more relevant if robots develop consciousness or emotional capacity. However, such a protection model could spark broader debates about whether robots should have rights equal to humans.

International regulations will play a crucial role in determining the legal status of robots. The global nature of technology requires the establishment of standards to ensure that robots have consistent rights and responsibilities across different countries. Such harmonization could contribute to the safer and more effective use of robots worldwide.

In conclusion, the legal statuses robots could hold will depend on technological advancements and the evolution of societal values. In this process, the impact of robots on humans, ethical boundaries, and societal expectations must be carefully considered. A well-designed legal framework can support the development of robots as tools that benefit humanity while minimizing potential risks.

6.2. DIGITAL WILLS AND ROBOTIC INTEGRATION

Digital wills, legal documents that outline how individuals wish to manage their digital assets and personal data after death, are becoming increasingly significant. With the rise of digital identities and robotic technologies, this concept has gained a new dimension. Questions about the role of digital copies and robotic systems after a person's death have sparked legal and ethical debates.

Digital wills may encompass social media accounts, digital archives, cloud-based files, and even the usage rights of digital copies. These documents specify who will control these assets and how they will be used after the individual's death. For example, decisions about whether a digital copy remains active, whether memories are shared with family members, or whether a digital archive is passed on as an inheritance can all be governed by digital wills.

Robotic integration is another critical aspect that must be considered within digital wills. After an individual's death, robotic entities can act as tools to carry out their wishes. For instance, a robot containing a person's memories and messages could form an emotional connection with family members and provide support during the grieving process. However, such integration raises complex ethical and emotional questions.

Digital wills and robotic integration also have significant implications for data security and privacy. Legal frameworks and security protocols are essential to prevent the misuse of an individual's digital copy or robotic systems. Ensuring these entities are used only for specified purposes and restricting access to third parties should be a key focus of legal regulations.

Ethically, digital wills ensure that individuals' posthumous wishes are respected. However, maintaining digital copies or robotic entities after death can impose emotional and psychological burdens on surviving family members. Therefore, when creating digital wills, individuals should consider not only their own desires but also the emotional well-being of their loved ones.

In conclusion, digital wills and robotic integration represent a critical intersection of technology and law. Legal frameworks that protect individual rights, respect ethical boundaries, and support the responsible use of technology are essential in this process. As digital wills become more widespread, they will enable individuals to manage their digital legacies more effectively and ensure that technology continues to serve as a meaningful tool for humanity.

6.2.1. Future Legal Regulations for Digital Copies

The development and expanding use of digital copies necessitate comprehensive legal frameworks to govern these technologies. Digital copies, capable of replicating an individual's personality, memories, and behaviors, introduce various legal dimensions such as privacy, ownership, and ethical responsibilities. Addressing these issues will be critical to ensuring the responsible and trustworthy use of this technology in the future.

The first priority is making explicit consent mandatory for the creation of digital copies. Legal regulations must ensure that a person's digital copy can only be created with their informed, voluntary, and explicit consent. This is a fundamental step in protecting individual rights and privacy.

Ownership and control of digital copies are also significant issues that require regulation. Determining who owns a digital copy and how it will be managed after the individual's death is particularly important for inheritance law. Legal frameworks should clarify whether these copies can be passed on to family members, designated heirs, or institutions.

Data security must be at the core of legal regulations concerning digital copies. Strict security standards should be enforced to protect digital copies from hacking or misuse. This not only safeguards individual rights but also impacts the broader role of these copies in society.

The commercial use of digital copies is another area that demands regulation. For instance, if a digital copy is used in advertising, education, or entertainment, the boundaries of this usage and how individual rights are protected must be clearly defined.

This aims to protect both the interests of individuals and uphold ethical standards.

Legal regulations should also address the societal impacts of digital copies. Policies must consider how these technologies will alter human relationships, labor markets, and social bonds, and aim to minimize negative consequences. This would promote the integration of technology in a socially harmonious manner.

The international dimension of digital copies should hold a special place in legal frameworks. Since digital technologies operate globally, it is necessary to establish a harmonized legal framework across countries. This ensures the protection of individual rights and data security on an international scale.

Ethical principles must be integrated into the legal regulations for digital copies. Legal frameworks should aim not only to protect individual rights but also to safeguard societal values and ethical standards. This guarantees that digital copies are used in ways that respect human dignity and rights.

In conclusion, the future legal regulations for digital copies require a comprehensive approach that balances individual rights, data security, and societal impacts. In this era of rapid technological advancement, legal systems must evolve to keep pace with these new realities. Such regulations can enable digital copies to be used in a beneficial, trustworthy, and ethical manner for humanity.

6.2.2. Inheritance Rights and Legal Responsibilities of Robotic Entities

The inheritance rights and legal responsibilities of robotic entities represent a new and complex area of law that has emerged alongside advances in technology. As robots gain human-like traits and develop autonomous decision-making capabilities, questions regarding their legal status become increasingly intricate. In particular, their potential inheritance rights and legal liabilities are key issues in this discussion.

Whether robots can have inheritance rights depends largely on their legal status. Under current legal frameworks, robots are considered property and therefore do not have inheritance rights like individuals. However, if robots were to gain legal personhood in the future, it might be possible for them to acquire certain rights, including inheritance, within the scope of legal frameworks.

If a robot were granted legal personhood, its inheritance rights could be defined as an extension of that status. For example, if a robot's owner dies, the question arises as to whether the robot could act as an independent entity capable of generating income or accumulating assets. However, such a development would require careful ethical and legal analysis.

The legal responsibilities of robotic entities become particularly significant when they are capable of autonomous actions. If a robot independently performs an action that causes harm, determining who is liable for the resulting damage is a critical question. Potential parties in such cases include the developers, owners, or possibly the robot itself.

Attributing independent responsibility to robots must be shaped not only by technical capabilities but also by ethical and legal standards. For instance, whether a robot could be held criminally liable, like a human, depends on the extent to which artificial intelligence can embody concepts such as consciousness and intent. Currently, robots are not considered to possess such capacities.

Another important aspect of inheritance and responsibilities involves whether robots can manage inherited assets on behalf of humans. For example, a robot could be tasked with preserving, managing, or distributing an estate as directed by its owner's will. This would position robots not just as tools but as reliable managers in specific roles.

An international approach to the inheritance rights and responsibilities of robotic entities is essential. The global nature of technology necessitates harmonized regulations across different countries. Such agreements would protect individual rights while also promoting the ethical and responsible use of robotics on a global scale.

In conclusion, the inheritance rights and legal responsibilities of robotic entities represent a novel and challenging area of law that accompanies technological advancements. Establishing clear and comprehensive legal frameworks will ensure the responsible use of this technology while maintaining justice within society. The future roles of robots will be shaped not only by technical capabilities but also by legal and ethical considerations.

6.3. INTERNATIONAL LEGAL REGULATIONS

The rapid globalization of technology and the widespread impact of digitalization have made international legal regulations more critical than ever. In fields such as artificial intelligence, robotic systems, digital copies, and data security, establishing global standards has become essential to ensure legal harmony between nations. These regulations aim to protect individual rights and promote the ethical and responsible use of technology.

One of the primary objectives of international legal regulations is to safeguard privacy and data security. Digital platforms and AI systems have the capacity to collect and process data on a global scale. Therefore, establishing unified data protection standards among countries is essential to prevent the misuse of personal information. The European Union's General Data Protection Regulation (GDPR) serves as a model, but similar frameworks should be adopted globally.

Robotic systems and AI applications also pose challenges for international law. For example, if an autonomous system crosses international borders and causes harm in another country, questions about liability and compensation arise. Such cases highlight the need to define how international law applies to cross-border technological incidents.

Digital copies and AI-related intellectual property rights require international regulation. For instance, who owns the intellectual property of a piece of art created by an AI system? Questions like these demand a standardized approach to intellectual property across nations. Such regulations could foster innovation while protecting individual rights.

International legal frameworks must also include ethical standards. Technological advancements bring ethical dilemmas that could impact societal values. Issues such as the use of robots in warfare, the impartiality of AI decision-making processes, and the ethical boundaries of digital copies should be addressed through international ethical norms.

Establishing global standards for AI and robotic technologies can also play a key role in reducing economic inequalities. Limiting access to technology to specific groups can exacerbate global inequalities. Therefore, international regulations should ensure that technology becomes accessible to a broader audience.

International legal regulations must also address technological developments in the military sphere. Autonomous weapon systems and AI-powered military tools could pose threats to global peace and security. Countries must collaborate to develop common protocols that define the ethical and legal limits of military technologies.

The effectiveness of these regulations depends on cooperation between nations. Given the borderless nature of technology, the implementation of international legal frameworks requires strong collaboration and communication mechanisms. This applies not only to states but also to international organizations and the private sector.

International legal systems should establish oversight mechanisms to monitor and ensure the responsible use of digital technologies on a global scale. These mechanisms can facilitate the effective enforcement of regulations and address violations swiftly.

In conclusion, international legal regulations are essential for ensuring the trustworthy, ethical, and responsible use of technology. Global cooperation and legal harmony are vital for achieving goals such as protecting individual rights, setting ethical standards, and reducing global inequalities. These regulations can ensure that technology serves as an opportunity rather than a threat to humanity.

6.3.1. Regulations on Digital Personalities and Robots in Different Countries

Different countries have adopted various approaches to regulate digital personalities and robots. These regulations aim to protect individual rights, establish ethical standards, and encourage innovation amid the rapid advancement of technology. However, the varying approaches across nations highlight the need for global harmonization and standardized frameworks.

The European Union (EU) has been at the forefront of regulations related to digital technologies and robotics. The General Data Protection Regulation (GDPR) is widely recognized as a global benchmark for protecting individuals' digital data. Additionally, the European Parliament has emphasized the need to establish ethical and legal frameworks for artificial intelligence (AI) and robotic systems. Issues such as the legal responsibility and autonomy of robots are being extensively debated within the EU.

Japan is one of the leading countries in robotics and has developed innovative regulations in this area. Robots are widely used in elder care and healthcare services in Japan. Regulations in these sectors aim to ensure the safety, ethical use, and integration of robots into society. The Japanese government has also developed a national framework to monitor the societal impacts of AI.

The United States takes a more market-driven approach to AI and robotics regulations. To encourage technological innovation, the U.S. generally implements flexible regulations for digital technologies and robots. However, there are discrepancies between states, leading to a lack of a consistent national framework. For example, California has stricter regulations regarding AI and data privacy, while other states adopt more lenient approaches.

China emphasizes the widespread adoption of AI and robotics, with regulations implemented under strict government control. The Chinese government has enacted comprehensive policies to enhance data security and surveillance systems. However, issues such as the ethical use of AI and the protection of individual rights receive less priority compared to international standards.

India is in the process of developing regulations for AI and robotic technologies. The use of AI in sectors like healthcare and education is on the rise. The Indian government has introduced guiding principles to assess the societal impacts of these technologies and ensure their ethical use. However, the scope of existing regulations is limited, and more comprehensive frameworks are needed.

In the United Kingdom, discussions around AI and robotic regulation have gained momentum. The government has proposed ethical principles to guide the development and use of these technologies, focusing on transparency, accountability, and fairness. The UK also emphasizes the need for public awareness and education regarding the societal implications of AI and robotics.

In conclusion, regulations concerning digital personalities and robots vary significantly across countries. While some nations are pioneering advancements in this area, others are still in the early stages of developing comprehensive legal frameworks. A globally unified and standardized approach is essential to ensure the ethical and secure use of these technologies. Such regulations would minimize the societal risks of emerging technologies while fostering innovation and collaboration on a global scale.

6.3.2. Global Cooperation and Standardization

The rapid development of technology and the global impact of digitalization have made international cooperation and standardization more critical than ever. Fields such as artificial intelligence, robotic systems, digital personalities, and data security require a unified approach to minimize the societal risks of cross-border technologies while fostering innovation and progress.

Global cooperation is essential for ensuring the ethical, secure, and equitable development and application of technology. Establishing shared objectives among nations provides a roadmap for maximizing the benefits of technology while mitigating its potential harms. This cooperation is particularly necessary to address global challenges arising from technology-driven issues.

Standardization serves as a vital tool for ensuring the consistent development of technology. International standards establish common criteria for transparency in AI algorithms, safety in robotic systems, and data management processes. These standards enable the consistent use and regulation of technology across different countries.

Global cooperation is particularly crucial in the areas of data security and privacy. Digital platforms and AI systems have the capacity to collect and process data worldwide. This requires the harmonization of data protection laws at an international level. Regulations like the European Union's GDPR can serve as a starting point for global collaboration.

Robotic systems and AI applications represent another key dimension of global cooperation. Autonomous systems that cross international borders and operate in different countries require common protocols for accountability and legal compliance. Such regulations ensure the seamless functionality of technology on an international scale.

Ethical standards are an integral part of global cooperation. Issues such as AI impartiality, the safety of robotic systems, and the misuse of digital copies demand universal ethical guidelines.

These principles can help ensure that technology is used for the benefit of humanity.

Global standardization also promotes broader access to technology. To prevent technological advancements from being concentrated in specific regions or among certain groups, an equitable approach at the international level is necessary. This can enhance fairness in technological access and help reduce economic inequalities.

International cooperation is particularly important in regulating the ethical use of military technologies. Autonomous weapons and AI-supported military tools pose risks to global security and peace. Therefore, common rules and boundaries must be established among nations to prevent the misuse of such technologies.

In conclusion, global cooperation and standardization are essential for the ethical and responsible use of technology. Strong collaborative mechanisms and shared standards among nations can minimize the negative impacts of technology on society while encouraging innovation. These efforts are key to creating a more equitable, secure, and sustainable technological future.

7. FUTURE SCENARIOS: HUMANITY AND HUMANOID ROBOTS

The development of humanoid robots presents a range of future scenarios, offering both opportunities and challenges for humanity. These scenarios revolve around the integration of robots into society, their interactions with humans, and the long-term impacts of technology on human life. As humanoid robots become more capable and assume broader roles, they may usher in one of the most significant transformations in human history.

The first scenario envisions humanoid robots as tools designed to simplify human life. Robots could take on active roles in healthcare, education, logistics, and household tasks. For example, they might provide care for the elderly, assist children with their education, or replace humans in dangerous jobs, significantly improving the quality of life.

The second scenario imagines humanoid robots as social entities. Robots capable of forming emotional connections, engaging in conversations, and demonstrating empathy could serve as companions for individuals suffering from loneliness. While this might alleviate isolation, it could also pose the risk of replacing genuine human relationships with artificial ones.

The third scenario involves humanoid robots becoming a significant part of the workforce. Robots might work alongside humans or even replace them in industries ranging from manufacturing to the service sector. While this could lead to dramatic increases in productivity, it may also result in societal issues like unemployment and income inequality. Humans may need to adapt to working with robots and redefine labor markets.

The fourth scenario explores robots as entities with ethical responsibilities. In this future, robots might be recognized as independent agents capable of making their own decisions and assuming responsibilities. However, this would require a reevaluation of their legal and ethical status. Questions about liability, such as who would be responsible if a robot caused harm, would become critical.

The fifth scenario focuses on the use of humanoid robots in military and security applications. Robots deployed in battlefields or for security operations could reduce human casualties. However, the ethical and legal dilemmas surrounding autonomous weapon systems present significant challenges in this context.

The sixth scenario envisions robots influencing human culture. Robots might contribute to creative fields such as art and literature, potentially reshaping cultural production. However, this could lead to debates about the value of human creativity in a world where machines play a significant role in cultural expression.

The seventh scenario suggests robots adapting to societal norms as if they were individuals. Robots might integrate into society by adopting cultural and ethical values, functioning as part of the community. This, however, raises ethical dilemmas about whether robots should be treated as real individuals.

The eighth scenario sees humanoid robots enhancing individual and societal freedoms. By taking over mundane tasks, robots could provide humans with more free time and opportunities for creative pursuits. Yet, this scenario also includes risks such as technological dependence and loss of control.

The ninth scenario envisions a class divide between humans and robots. If advanced technology becomes accessible only to certain groups, it could deepen social inequalities. This underscores the importance of global regulations to ensure technology is distributed ethically and equitably.

The tenth scenario explores deeper human-robot relationships. Romantic or familial bonds with humanoid robots could redefine human emotional dynamics. However, this could challenge traditional societal norms and provoke debates about the nature of human relationships.

In conclusion, the future scenarios involving humanoid robots depend on how technology is directed and how society responds to these changes. While robots offer vast opportunities, they also bring complex ethical, legal, and societal issues. The future will be shaped by how these opportunities and challenges are managed.

7.1. THE IMPACT OF HUMANOID ROBOTS ON SOCIAL TRANSFORMATION

The development of humanoid robots is seen as a pivotal moment in social transformation. These robots not only introduce technological innovations but also profoundly influence social, economic, and cultural structures. With their ability to mimic human behavior and interact with people, humanoid robots have the potential to establish new norms in various areas of societal life.

The first significant impact is on the workforce. Robots can increase efficiency in production and service sectors and replace human workers in dangerous jobs. However, this may lead to higher unemployment rates and the disappearance of certain professions. People may need to acquire new skills to compete with robots, reshaping labor markets.

Second, humanoid robots could alter interpersonal social interactions. Robots capable of engaging in conversation and forming emotional bonds could provide companionship to individuals experiencing loneliness. However, this might result in weakened social bonds if human relationships are replaced by interactions with robots. Younger generations, in particular, might develop reduced attachment to real human relationships due to increased reliance on robots.

Third, humanoid robots hold the potential to revolutionize critical areas such as education and healthcare. Robots can provide personalized learning experiences, transforming education, and assist in various healthcare services, from elder care to rehabilitation. While these advancements could enhance societal well-being, they also raise ethical concerns about the boundaries of human-robot interactions.

Humanoid robots may also influence cultural values and norms. Their involvement in creative fields like art, literature, and media could challenge traditional notions of human creativity. Additionally, perceptions of robots may vary across cultures, potentially reshaping societal norms in different ways.

Economically, humanoid robots could lower production costs and pave the way for new business models. However, this might disadvantage small businesses that struggle to compete with large technology companies, exacerbating economic inequalities. Social policies may be necessary to mitigate these disparities and ensure equitable access to technological benefits.

Ethically, questions arise regarding whether humanoid robots should be afforded protections similar to human rights. Issues such as banning the abuse of robots or granting them certain rights could reshape societal ethical frameworks. Additionally, human responsibilities toward robots may become part of social dynamics.

In conclusion, the impact of humanoid robots on social transformation is multifaceted and depends on how technology is implemented and how society responds to these changes. While robots offer opportunities in various areas, they also bring complex challenges and ethical dilemmas. Careful planning and regulation are essential to ensure that the effects of humanoid robots on social transformation remain positive and beneficial for humanity.

7.1.2. The Role of Robots in Education, Healthcare, and Business

The role of robots in education, healthcare, and business has become increasingly significant with the rapid advancement of technology. In these sectors, robots have the potential to enhance efficiency and create more opportunities for people. However, this transformation also brings ethical, economic, and societal challenges.

In education, robots can provide personalized learning experiences by tailoring the educational environment to the individual needs of students. Robotic tutors can assist with language learning, mathematics, and other core subjects. Moreover, AI-powered robots can analyze students' strengths and weaknesses to optimize their learning processes.

Another crucial role of robots in education is promoting inclusivity. Robots designed for students with physical disabilities can provide accessible learning tools. For example, robotic systems tailored for individuals with hearing or visual impairments can contribute to equity in education.

In healthcare, robots play a significant role in diagnosis and treatment processes. Robotic surgical systems enable more precise operations and reduce the likelihood of errors. Rehabilitation robots can accelerate physical therapy and offer personalized treatment based on individual patient needs.

Another critical contribution of robots in healthcare is reducing the workload of medical staff. Robots can assist with managing patient records, distributing medication, and performing routine tasks, allowing healthcare workers to spend more time with patients and focus on complex responsibilities.

In business, robots increase automation in production processes, reducing costs and boosting efficiency. In repetitive and physically demanding tasks, robots can replace human labor, lowering workplace accidents. This allows businesses to operate more safely and effectively.

Robots also contribute to the development of innovative business models. For instance, AI-powered robots can be used in data analysis, customer service, and marketing, helping companies make better decisions. This provides a competitive edge and contributes to business growth.

However, the growing role of robots in business could lead to significant transformations in the labor market. The full automation of certain professions may increase unemployment rates and deepen economic inequalities. As a result, there will be a growing need for reskilling and upskilling programs to help workers adapt to new technologies.

The role of robots in these three areas has the potential to enhance overall societal well-being. However, responsible use of these technologies and preventive measures for potential negative impacts will require comprehensive regulations and ethical guidelines. Proper management of technology can yield significant benefits for individuals and society alike.

In conclusion, robots have the potential to revolutionize education, healthcare, and business. This transformation will not only improve the quality of services but also reshape societal structures. To maximize the positive effects of this technological advancement, a balanced approach should be adopted, and human-robot collaboration should be utilized in the most efficient way.

7.1.3. The Future of Human-Machine Interactions

The future of human-machine interactions holds the potential to drive profound changes across all areas of life, fueled by rapid technological advancements. The deepening relationship between humans and machines will reshape individual experiences and societal structures, accelerating with developments in artificial intelligence, robotics, and user-friendly technologies.

Artificial intelligence (AI) will play a central role in the future of human-machine interactions. AI systems can analyze and learn from human behavior, offering personalized services that improve efficiency in healthcare, education, business, and beyond.

This will enable humans to interact with machines in a more natural and intuitive manner.

Emotional connections between humans and machines may also become a significant aspect of these interactions. The development of humanoid robots can strengthen these bonds. Emotionally intelligent systems capable of understanding human emotional states and responding appropriately could lead to machines being perceived not just as tools but as "partners."

In the business world, human-machine interactions have the potential to revolutionize productivity. Employees working alongside robotic systems are expected to achieve higher levels of efficiency. For instance, robots can take over repetitive tasks in factories, allowing humans to focus on creative and strategic roles. However, this shift will also lead to significant transformations in labor markets.

In education, interactions with machines can transform individual learning experiences. Robotic tutors and AI-driven learning platforms can provide flexible, personalized education tailored to students' needs. This could promote greater equity in education by expanding access to opportunities for diverse societal groups.

In healthcare, human-machine interactions are already transforming diagnosis and treatment processes. From robotic surgery to AI-powered diagnostic systems, machines are improving the accuracy and speed of healthcare services. In the future, direct relationships between patients and robots could make healthcare more accessible and human-centric.

In daily life, human-machine interactions are becoming increasingly commonplace. Smart home systems, voice assistants, and wearable technologies enable continuous interaction with machines to meet everyday needs. These technologies have the potential to make life more comfortable and convenient.

Ethically, the future of human-machine interactions raises critical questions. Issues such as human privacy, data security, and the impartiality of machine decision-making must be addressed to define the boundaries of these interactions. Resolving these challenges can minimize the negative societal impacts of advancing technology.

Culturally, interactions with machines may lead to changes in societal norms and values. The perception and acceptance of machines vary across cultures, which will play a crucial role in shaping these interactions. Cultural awareness and local values will be key to the adoption of technology.

At an international level, regulating and standardizing human-machine interactions will become increasingly necessary. The global nature of technology requires inclusive and harmonized frameworks across different countries. This can ensure that technology is used in a reliable and ethical manner worldwide.

In conclusion, the future of human-machine interactions will depend on the pace of technology and society's ability to adapt to these changes. These interactions have the potential to improve quality of life, enhance efficiency, and create new opportunities. However, addressing the ethical, social, and economic challenges will be critical.

In a future where humans and machines collaborate, directing technology in a human-centered way can provide a better life for both individuals and society. A balanced approach must be adopted to maximize the positive impacts of human-machine interactions and ensure that everyone benefits from this technological transformation.

7.2. UTOPIA OR DYSTOPIA?

The rapid advancement of technology and the widespread integration of digitalization into every aspect of life raise a critical question: will the future be a utopia or a dystopia? Innovations in artificial intelligence, humanoid robots, and digital systems offer humanity immense opportunities while simultaneously presenting ethical, social, and economic risks. The balance between these possibilities depends on how technology is utilized and directed.

In a utopian scenario, technology could serve as a tool to enhance the quality of human life. Robots could take over dangerous and monotonous tasks, allowing humans to focus on creative and meaningful endeavors. Artificial intelligence could help achieve equality in essential services like healthcare and education, boosting societal welfare. Technology could also break down barriers, fostering stronger global cooperation and understanding.

Conversely, in a dystopian scenario, the misuse of technology could pose significant threats to humanity. Unregulated use of autonomous weapons could jeopardize global security. Furthermore, artificial intelligence could exacerbate social inequalities, widening economic divides. Job losses and the weakening of social bonds might reveal the darker side of technological progress.

The potential for technology to create a utopia or dystopia is closely tied to ethical boundaries and regulations. Respect for human rights, data security, and environmental sustainability are essential principles for ensuring the responsible use of technology. If these principles are ignored, technology could lead society into deeper problems. However, with proper guidance, technology can become an unparalleled opportunity for progress.

In conclusion, whether the future leans towards utopia or dystopia will depend on our approach to technology. Adopting a human-centered technological perspective can transform technology from a threat into an opportunity. Striking the right balance requires safeguarding ethical values and human dignity while directing technological progress. Technology represents one of humanity's greatest tests, holding both immense hope and profound responsibility.

7.2.1. The Potential Benefits and Risks of Digital Immortality and Humanoid Robots

Digital immortality and humanoid robots are among the most controversial and promising innovations of modern technology. The concept of sustaining human consciousness in digital environments and integrating it with humanoid robots could have groundbreaking effects on both individual and societal levels. However, alongside their potential benefits, these technologies also pose significant risks that must be carefully considered.

Digital immortality offers the possibility of preserving memories, personality traits, and consciousness digitally, enabling individuals to "exist" in some form even after physical death. This could provide emotional support to grieving loved ones by allowing them to interact with a digital copy of the deceased, potentially easing the mourning process.

When combined with humanoid robots, digital immortality could create a physical extension of an individual's digital self. For example, transferring a digital copy into a robot would allow it to act as a representation of the person, both physically and mentally. This could provide invaluable assistance in fields such as education, healthcare, and counseling.

Digital immortality also presents a unique opportunity to pass on human knowledge and experience to future generations. By digitally recording a lifetime's worth of information and insights, individuals could contribute to education and research, expanding humanity's collective memory and understanding.

Humanoid robots, beyond their individual capabilities, hold significant potential for societal benefits. Robots can be used effectively in critical areas such as elder care, healthcare, and disaster management. For instance, in aging societies, humanoid robots could provide personal care and support to elderly individuals, addressing growing caregiving needs.

However, these technologies also come with considerable risks. Digital immortality could threaten privacy. The misuse of a person's digital copy could lead to data security breaches and ethical violations. Especially when used for commercial purposes, digital copies may infringe on individual rights.

The widespread use of humanoid robots may lead to significant disruptions in the labor market. As robots replace human workers, unemployment rates could rise, deepening economic inequalities. This could create social unrest and imbalance in income distribution.

Another risk is the potential replacement of human relationships with interactions with humanoid robots. Emotional bonds with robots could weaken genuine human connections, leading to increased loneliness and a breakdown of traditional social structures.

Ethically, digital immortality and humanoid robots raise complex questions. Issues such as whether robots should be granted rights similar to human rights and what responsibilities humans have toward robots could reshape societal ethical frameworks.

The misuse of these technologies poses further risks. Authoritarian regimes might exploit digital immortality and humanoid robots to control societies or restrict individual freedoms, highlighting the darker side of technological advancement.

The environmental impact of these technologies must also be considered. The production of humanoid robots and the energy consumption of digital platforms could pose challenges to environmental sustainability. Innovative solutions will be needed to minimize the ecological footprint of these technologies.

Digital immortality could also alter humanity's perception of death. The concept of physical death no longer being a definitive end may lead to profound changes in religious, philosophical, and cultural beliefs, prompting societies to redefine spiritual values.

The integration of digital immortality with humanoid robots could affect individuals' sense of identity. People might question whether their digital copies fully represent their true selves, potentially leading to identity crises and psychological challenges.

The legal frameworks surrounding digital copies and humanoid robots will be crucial for shaping the future of these technologies. Comprehensive regulations addressing issues like data security, ownership rights, and accountability are necessary to manage the complexities of this new era.

In conclusion, digital immortality and humanoid robots represent both incredible opportunities and significant risks for humanity. Proper guidance and regulation are essential to ensure that these technologies benefit society. Ethical and responsible use of technology is critical to mitigating its potential negative impacts.

Digital immortality and humanoid robots signify one of the most transformative shifts in human history. These advancements have the power to redefine the meaning of being human and reshape societal structures. However, for this transformation to be positive, technology must be directed to serve humanity's best interests.

7.2.2. New Opportunities and Threats for Humanity

Technological advancements present humanity with both great opportunities and significant threats. Developments in artificial intelligence, robotics, digitalization, and biotechnology have the potential to enhance the quality of life while simultaneously introducing societal, economic, and ethical challenges. These opportunities and threats will shape the future of humanity depending on how technology is used and directed.

Among the opportunities, the transformation of healthcare stands out. Robotic surgery, AI-powered diagnostic systems, and telemedicine offer faster and more precise treatment options. Additionally, genetic engineering and biotechnology could revolutionize the prevention and treatment of diseases, potentially extending human life spans.

In education, technological innovations provide immense possibilities. Artificial intelligence and online learning platforms enable personalized educational experiences, allowing students to learn at their own pace. Moreover, virtual and augmented reality technologies make it easier to teach and understand complex subjects effectively.

Economically, technological progress creates new job opportunities and industries. The development of AI and robotic systems fosters innovation and optimizes business processes. This reduces production costs while enabling the emergence of more efficient and sustainable business models.

However, these opportunities come with serious threats. The impact of technology on the workforce could lead to the disappearance of many professions due to automation. Workers in low-skill jobs are likely to be the most affected, resulting in higher unemployment rates and deepening income inequality.

Technological dependency is another major threat. As people become increasingly reliant on technology in almost every aspect of their daily lives, this dependency could limit individual freedoms. Excessive use of social media and digital platforms, for instance, can lead to psychological issues and social isolation.

Privacy and data security concerns represent another significant danger of digitalization. The misuse of personal data can violate individual rights. Control of this data by large tech companies or authoritarian regimes may lead to increased societal surveillance and repression.

Ethically, the misuse of technology poses critical risks. Autonomous weapon systems, genetic manipulation, or unchecked use of artificial intelligence could threaten human rights and escalate global security risks. These challenges underline the importance of ethical guidelines and international regulations.

Environmental impacts are another threat posed by technology. The production of technological devices and energy consumption can lead to the depletion of natural resources and increased pollution. Without sustainable technological solutions, these effects could exacerbate global crises such as climate change.

In conclusion, the opportunities and threats posed by technology represent a critical crossroads for humanity's future. With the right policies, ethical principles, and international cooperation, it is possible to harness the benefits of these advancements while minimizing their risks. When used as a tool for humanity, technology has the potential to create a more just, sustainable, and inclusive future.

7.3. THE NEW DEFINITION OF BEING HUMAN

In our rapidly advancing technological era, the meaning of being human is undergoing a profound redefinition. Innovations in artificial intelligence, humanoid robots, genetic engineering, and digital immortality are reshaping individuals' sense of identity, their roles in society, and the purpose of life. Humanity is no longer defined solely as a biological entity but as one deeply intertwined with digital and technological systems.

Traditionally, being human has been associated with qualities such as consciousness, emotion, creativity, and ethical responsibility. However, as artificial intelligence and robotics increasingly simulate these traits, the uniqueness of these human characteristics is being questioned. A robot capable of human-like behavior or an AI capable of producing creative content challenges the boundaries of what it means to be human.

Technological advancements are also pushing the limits of human biology. Through genetic engineering and biotechnology, humans can potentially prevent diseases, enhance physical capabilities, and extend lifespans. This blurs the line between the "natural human" and the "engineered human," prompting a reevaluation of what it truly means to be human.

The concept of digital immortality further transforms the definition of being human. The possibility of transferring human consciousness to a digital environment offers a form of existence beyond physical life. This suggests that humans are not just physical beings but entities whose knowledge and experiences can persist in a digital format.

In the new definition of humanity, interaction with technology plays a central role. People are now forming emotional and social bonds not only with other humans but also with AI and robots. These interactions are reshaping human roles within social structures and raising ethical questions about human-robot relationships.

The redefinition of humanity also encompasses our relationship with the environment and technology. Building a sustainable future requires humans to manage their impact on nature more consciously. Technology can redefine humanity's role in this process by increasing individual and societal responsibility toward the environment.

From an ethical and philosophical perspective, the new definition of being human raises debates about individual freedom, rights, and responsibilities. Questions such as whether human rights should extend to digital entities or whether robots can possess rights challenge traditional notions of humanity and expand its boundaries.

In conclusion, the new definition of being human integrates biological, digital, and ethical dimensions. Technology's impact on humanity continuously reshapes what it means to be human. Preserving human essence and values while using technology for the benefit of humanity will be a crucial element of this evolving definition.

7.3.1. How Digitalization and Robotic Developments Are Changing the Perception of Being Human

Digitalization and advancements in robotics are profoundly transforming the perception of being human. Traditionally, humanity has been defined by qualities such as consciousness, emotions, creativity, and ethical responsibility. However, digital and robotic innovations are challenging these boundaries, reshaping humanity as not just a biological entity but one that can also exist within digital platforms and robotic systems.

Artificial intelligence (AI) has disrupted traditional notions of uniquely human traits. AI's ability to mimic human behaviors, solve problems, and even exhibit creativity raises questions about whether being human can be defined solely by such capabilities. This challenges the idea that these traits are exclusive to humans, prompting a reevaluation of what it truly means to be human.

Digitalization has redefined the concept of identity. Social media, digital profiles, and virtual reality environments allow individuals to create digital representations of themselves. Today, a person is not only defined by their physical presence but also by the digital footprints they leave behind. This evolution extends the concept of identity beyond biological existence.

Robotic advancements have expanded the physical limits of humanity. Robotic prosthetics, augmented reality tools, and human-machine integration enhance physical capabilities, enabling humans to transcend biological boundaries. These technologies normalize the idea of surpassing natural limitations, altering the traditional understanding of the human body.

The concept of digital immortality has revolutionized perceptions of human existence. The ability to digitally transfer consciousness, memories, and personality traits introduces the idea of continued existence beyond physical death. This suggests that humans are not confined to a finite biological lifespan but can persist as digital entities.

The development of humanoid robots is reshaping humanity's role in society. Robots capable of forming emotional connections and engaging in social interactions raise ethical questions about human-robot relationships. The nature of these interactions challenges the boundaries of what it means to be human.

Digitalization has also transformed the perception of creativity. AI-powered systems producing art, literature, and music demonstrate that creativity is not solely a human attribute. This forces a reevaluation of humanity's unique role in cultural production.

Robotic and digital advancements have broadened ethical responsibilities. Humans are now accountable not only to other humans but also to robots and digital entities. This expansion of ethical obligations necessitates the development of new ethical frameworks to address the complexities of these relationships.

Privacy and data security have become central to the evolving perception of humanity in the digital age. The misuse of personal data forces individuals to reconsider their rights and boundaries in the digital world. People must adapt to new ways of protecting and representing themselves in an increasingly digital environment.

Digitalization and robotics also provoke questions about the purpose of human existence. In a world where robots can potentially replace humans, the meaning and value of individual contributions are being reexamined. This compels humanity to redefine itself and assign new meaning to its existence.

In conclusion, digitalization and robotic advancements are reshaping the perception of being human in profound ways. Humanity is no longer seen solely as a biological entity but as one that exists within digital and technological dimensions. This transformation presents both opportunities and challenges at individual and societal levels, continuously redefining the essence of what it means to be human.

7.3.2. The Ultimate Impact of Technology on Humanity

The ultimate impact of technology on humanity holds the power to transform every aspect of human life. While it promises to enhance the quality of life, strengthen communication, and make societies more interconnected, it also brings complex ethical, social, and environmental challenges. How technology is directed will ultimately determine its effects on humanity.

First, technology has expanded human boundaries, enhancing both physical and mental capabilities. Artificial intelligence, robotics, and biotechnology have made people more productive, creative, and resilient. For instance, technological advancements in healthcare have revolutionized human life by extending lifespans and enabling the treatment of once-fatal diseases.

However, technology has also profoundly influenced human relationships. While social media and digital platforms have made communication easier, they have also reduced face-to-face interactions and increased feelings of isolation. The psychological effects of the digital world are one of the most complex aspects of technology's impact on humanity.

Technology can both bridge and widen societal inequalities. It has the potential to make essential services like education and healthcare more accessible, promoting equality for certain communities. At the same time, the exclusivity of advanced technologies to specific groups can deepen economic and social divides. Therefore, ensuring equitable access to technology is critical to maximizing its positive impact on humanity.

From an ethical perspective, technology's ultimate impact on humanity raises significant debates. Issues such as whether artificial intelligence can make unbiased decisions or whether robots should have rights challenge traditional human values and ethical frameworks. Guiding technology responsibly and ethically is essential to achieving outcomes that benefit humanity.

Environmentally, technology can exacerbate problems such as climate change and pollution by increasing the consumption of natural resources. On the other hand, renewable energy and eco-friendly technologies hold the potential to address environmental issues. Managing the environmental impact of technology is key to building a sustainable future for humanity.

In conclusion, the ultimate impact of technology on humanity represents a delicate balance that transforms human nature and societal structures. To harness its positive effects and minimize its negative consequences, ethical guidelines, regulations, and international cooperation are necessary. Humanity must learn to use technology not only as a tool but as a means to uphold and advance human values.

8. CONCLUSION: HUMANITY'S DIGITAL FUTURE

Digitalization represents a transformative process for humanity, bringing both immense opportunities and complex challenges. At this critical juncture in history, technology has evolved from being a tool for convenience to a force that reshapes human identity, societal structures, and value systems. This process demands a redefinition of humanity at both individual and collective levels.

The digital future of humanity is driving profound changes in the concept of identity. Tools like social media, digital identities, and virtual reality have diversified how individuals express themselves. People are now defined not only by their physical presence but also by the digital traces they leave behind. This has rendered identity dynamic and multidimensional.

Digitalization has also expanded the biological boundaries of human life. Innovations such as genetic engineering, biotechnology, and artificial organs have extended lifespans and enhanced physical capabilities. However, transcending the limits of the human body has sparked philosophical and ethical debates about the essence of being human.

Artificial intelligence and robotic systems challenge humanity's cognitive and emotional uniqueness. AI's competence in learning, decision-making, and creative processes raises questions about the exclusivity of human traits. This complicates humanity's relationship with technology and necessitates the adoption of new responsibilities and roles.

In the digital future, societal structures are undergoing transformation. Technology's impact on the labor market has redefined professions, with many jobs becoming automated. Humans must learn to collaborate with robots and adapt to evolving economic conditions.

In fundamental areas such as education and healthcare, digitalization offers significant opportunities. Digital tools and AI-driven systems can provide tailored services that promote equity. However, if access to technology is limited to specific groups, it could exacerbate social inequalities. Ensuring the fair distribution of technology is therefore crucial.

The digitalization process is also altering humanity's relationship with the environment. The environmental impacts of technology, including resource consumption and climate change, have sparked critical debates. Developing environmentally friendly technologies will play a decisive role in achieving a sustainable future for humanity.

Ethically, humanity faces new challenges in a digitalized future. Issues such as the ethical use of AI and robots, digital rights, and privacy compel societies to reconsider their value systems. Integrating ethical principles into technological frameworks is essential for navigating this era responsibly.

The development of digital immortality and humanoid robots redefines human existence. The ability to sustain human consciousness on digital platforms and integrate it with robotic systems suggests a perception of humanity that transcends physical limitations. Yet, these innovations also raise profound questions about the core of human essence.

Digitalization has also impacted human relationships. While technology has enhanced connectivity, it has also reduced face-to-face interactions and increased dependence on the digital world. This highlights the importance of finding a balance between technology and humanity to preserve social cohesion.

Humanity's digital future necessitates global cooperation and regulation. The global nature of technology requires governance not only at national levels but also through international collaboration. Such efforts are crucial to prevent the misuse of technology and to amplify its positive effects.

In conclusion, digitalization has opened doors to a future filled with new opportunities and challenges. Humanity bears the responsibility of preserving its essence while directing technology for the benefit of society. This process will redefine the meaning of being human, driving profound transformation on both individual and societal levels.

Humanity's digital future requires an ethical, sustainable, and inclusive approach to fully harness the potential of technology. This transformation carries the promise of creating a fairer and more meaningful world while safeguarding humanity's core values.

8.1. THE IMPORTANCE OF DIGITAL IMMORTALITY FOR HUMANITY

Digital immortality represents a modern technological response to humanity's age-old quest for eternal life. The ability to transfer human consciousness, memories, and personality into digital platforms enables humanity to transcend biological limitations. This concept holds profound potential to create transformative impacts on both individual and societal levels.

One of the most significant contributions of digital immortality is the possibility for individuals to continue existing in some form after their physical death. When a person's memories, values, and thoughts are digitized, this knowledge can serve as a guide for future generations. It shows that humans are not merely biological beings but entities whose information and experiences can endure.

Digital immortality can provide emotional support during the grieving process. A digital copy of a loved one could allow the bereaved to interact with or keep the memories of the deceased alive. This can make the mourning period more meaningful and bearable.

From an educational perspective, digital immortality offers unique opportunities. Preserving accumulated knowledge and experiences in digital form can expand humanity's collective memory. Digital representations of past scientists, philosophers, or artists could inspire and educate future generations.

Digital immortality also redefines the perception of individual identity. The possibility of existing beyond the physical body allows individuals to view themselves from a broader perspective.

This can lead to new meanings and values being attributed to human existence.

On a societal level, digital immortality can contribute to preserving cultural diversity. Traditions, languages, and knowledge from different cultures can be stored on digital platforms, safeguarding them from being forgotten. This helps provide a more comprehensive understanding of human history for future generations.

Digital immortality extends humanity's efforts to overcome biological constraints. Goals such as preventing diseases or slowing aging gain a broader dimension through the concept of digital immortality. It is part of humanity's search to enhance the value of life and pursue a meaningful existence for longer periods.

However, digital immortality brings not only opportunities but also ethical and societal questions. Issues such as the rights of digital copies, protection of privacy, and prevention of misuse are critical for the viability of this technology. Thus, digital immortality must be supported by ethical frameworks.

Another significant aspect of digital immortality is its potential to reshape the relationship between humans and machines. When a person's digital consciousness is integrated into a robot, this robot can become a reflection of the individual both physically and mentally. This could usher in a new era of human-robot interactions.

Digital immortality could also play an important role in business. Preserving the knowledge and expertise of leaders or specialists digitally could ensure the continuity of organizations. This provides a significant advantage in maintaining institutional memory.

In healthcare, digital immortality could support personalized treatment and rehabilitation processes. A person's digital consciousness could guide healthcare professionals by offering comprehensive insights into the patient's history and needs. This would enhance the effectiveness and success of medical treatments.

Digital immortality also raises philosophical questions about human existence. The ability to exist beyond the physical body may lead individuals to reevaluate concepts of life and death. This could result in profound changes in their spiritual and psychological outlook.

Environmentally, digital immortality may contribute to more efficient use of resources. Opting for digital existence over physical forms could reduce energy consumption and lessen the burden on the environment. However, ensuring the sustainability of digital infrastructure is equally crucial.

Digital immortality is a milestone in humanity's journey to explore its potential. It has expanded the way humans perceive themselves and the world. This technological innovation represents a transformation unlike anything humanity has experienced before.

In conclusion, digital immortality is a transformative force for humanity. It has the potential to redefine human identity, relationships, and values on both individual and societal levels. Maximizing its positive impacts requires an ethical, legal, and sustainable approach to ensure a secure digital future for humanity.

8.1.1. Humanity's Adaptation to Artificial Intelligence and Robots

The rapid advancement of artificial intelligence (AI) and robotics is profoundly affecting human life, making adaptation to these technologies a necessity. For humans to live harmoniously with AI and robots, new skills, values, and understandings must be developed on both individual and societal levels. This adaptation process encompasses not only technological aspects but also ethical, psychological, and sociological dimensions.

The first step in adapting to AI and robots is raising awareness about their use. Understanding how AI operates, its potential, and its limitations can build trust in these technologies. Educational and awareness programs can help individuals interact with AI and robots more effectively.

Adaptation to AI and robots is particularly significant in the workplace. With the rise of automation, many professions have been transformed or eliminated entirely. To adapt to these changes, individuals must acquire new skills and pivot toward creative and innovative fields. This underscores the importance of lifelong learning.

A critical aspect of adaptation is establishing ethical guidelines for human-machine interactions. Ensuring fairness in AI decision-making processes, protecting data security, and respecting individual privacy will foster harmony between humans and robots. An ethical framework is also essential for building public trust in these technologies.

Psychological adaptation is another important factor in harmonizing with AI and robots. People must become accustomed to the presence of robots and view them as part of their daily lives. However, it is crucial to prevent robotic relationships from replacing human-to-human connections. Emotional needs should primarily be fulfilled through genuine social bonds rather than through technology.

The education sector plays a pivotal role in fostering human-robot harmony. AI-powered educational tools can optimize learning processes for individuals. However, ensuring fair and accessible use of these technologies in education is vital for everyone to benefit equally from this transformation.

In healthcare, human-robot collaboration can greatly improve treatment processes. Robotic surgical systems, AI-assisted diagnostic tools, and care robots can make healthcare services more efficient. However, the ethical boundaries of patient-robot interactions must be clearly defined.

The adaptation to AI and robots also impacts social structures. Increased interactions with robots in the workplace and daily life may reshape societal norms and values. Inclusivity and consideration of diverse perspectives are essential for developing solutions that address the needs of all societal groups.

Adaptation is not only required of individuals and societies but also of technology developers. Designing AI and robots with a human-centered approach ensures these technologies better meet human needs. Developing user-friendly technologies can significantly ease the adaptation process.

Economically, adapting to AI and robots plays a crucial role in achieving sustainable development goals. These technologies can enhance efficiency and reduce costs, contributing to economic growth. However, policies must be established to ensure the fair distribution of these benefits.

Environmental considerations are another important dimension of human-robot adaptation. The production of robots and the energy consumption of AI systems must be carefully managed to maintain environmental sustainability. Developing eco-friendly technologies can help minimize the negative environmental impacts of this process.

In conclusion, humanity's adaptation to AI and robots is a multidimensional and dynamic process. This adaptation enables technology to improve the quality of human life while addressing ethical, social, and environmental responsibilities. Striking a balance between humans and machines is a critical step in using technology for the betterment of humanity.

8.1.2. The New Opportunities Offered by Technology

The rapid advancement of technology has created numerous new opportunities for humanity. These opportunities have the potential to enhance individual quality of life while transforming societal structures, economic activities, and global cooperation. However, realizing the full potential of these opportunities depends on proper usage and guidance.

One of the greatest opportunities technology offers is access to information. The internet and digital platforms enable individuals around the world to instantly access knowledge. In areas such as education and scientific research, this accessibility enriches knowledge and promotes equality.

In the healthcare sector, technology has revolutionized diagnosis and treatment processes. AI-powered systems facilitate early detection of diseases, while innovations like robotic surgery make treatments more precise. Additionally, telemedicine applications allow individuals in remote areas to access quality healthcare services.

Economically, technology has created new industries and job opportunities. Fields such as artificial intelligence, robotics, and data analytics provide innovative career paths for individuals and businesses. Technology also optimizes work processes, increasing productivity and reducing costs.

In education, technology offers personalized learning opportunities. Online education platforms and AI-driven teaching tools enable students to learn at their own pace. This increased accessibility strengthens the foundation of a knowledge-based society.

Technology also presents significant opportunities in sustainability and environmental protection. Renewable energy technologies help reduce carbon footprints, while smart city systems promote more efficient use of resources. These advancements support global efforts to address environmental challenges.

Social media and digital communication tools make it easier for individuals and communities to connect. People can engage with diverse cultures and create networks that transcend borders. This fosters global cooperation and understanding, which are vital in today's interconnected world.

Technology has also transformed how individuals express their creativity. Digital art, content creation, and virtual reality have opened new avenues for modern artists and creators. This has led to greater diversity and innovation in cultural production.

In business, data analytics and big data technologies enable companies to make better decisions. Analyzing consumer behavior, predicting market trends, and improving operational efficiency are just a few of the opportunities these technologies provide.

Finally, technology offers solutions that save time in daily life. Smart home devices, automation systems, and personal assistants make everyday tasks easier and more efficient. This allows individuals to dedicate more time to creative and meaningful activities.

The opportunities provided by technology have the potential to transform every aspect of human life. Ensuring these opportunities are distributed fairly and supported by ethical principles is key to making technology beneficial for all of humanity.

8.2. TECHNOLOGY AND RESPONSIBILITY

The rapid advancement of technology brings new opportunities and solutions for humanity while simultaneously introducing significant responsibilities. These responsibilities extend to individuals, governments, corporations, and civil society. The effective and ethical use of technology requires a strong sense of responsibility at both individual and societal levels.

At the individual level, ethical behavior when using technology is essential. Sharing accurate information on digital platforms, protecting personal data, and respecting others' rights are key elements of responsible technology use. Additionally, individuals must manage risks such as technology addiction and ensure they use technology in ways that enhance, rather than harm, their lives.

For corporations, technological responsibility involves prioritizing societal benefit alongside profitability. Companies developing technology must ensure their products do not violate human rights, harm the environment, or exacerbate social inequalities. Furthermore, in fields such as artificial intelligence and data analytics, transparency and fairness should be fundamental principles.

Governments play a regulatory role in ensuring the responsible use of technology. Establishing legal frameworks for data security, privacy, and the ethical use of artificial intelligence is a critical responsibility of governments. Additionally, promoting equal access to technology and implementing social policies to prevent societal divisions are essential components of their duties.

The environmental impact of technology is another crucial area of responsibility. The production of technological devices and their energy consumption can negatively affect the environment. Both individuals and institutions must shift towards environmentally friendly technologies and adhere to sustainability principles to mitigate these impacts.

In conclusion, technology and responsibility are two interconnected concepts. Transforming technology from a potential threat into an opportunity for humanity is only possible through ethical and responsible approaches. By fostering a shared understanding among individuals, corporations, and governments, technology can be used in a way that is sustainable, equitable, and beneficial for all.

8.2.1. Ethical Boundaries and Social Awareness

Technological advancements offer significant opportunities to improve and simplify human life, but these advancements must remain within ethical boundaries to ensure their responsible use. Ethical boundaries help ensure that technology respects human rights, is environmentally sustainable, and promotes social harmony. Maintaining these boundaries requires all stakeholders, from individuals to global organizations, to develop and embrace social awareness.

The most fundamental aspect of ethical boundaries is the protection of individual rights. The widespread use of technology, particularly in data collection and processing, raises critical concerns about personal data security and privacy. Big data analytics and AI applications store and analyze vast amounts of personal information. An ethical approach demands that such data be used only with explicit consent and securely protected from misuse.

Social awareness plays a critical role in upholding ethical values in the use of technology. Understanding the potential harms of technology and fostering awareness among the public is the first step in preventing ethical violations. For example, responsible behavior on digital platforms, such as sharing accurate information and avoiding hate speech, is a key aspect of individual responsibility.

For corporations, ethical boundaries require prioritizing societal benefits alongside profitability. Technology companies must consider human rights, environmental sustainability, and social balance when developing their products and services. For instance, AI algorithms must be designed to be unbiased and avoid perpetuating discrimination as part of their ethical responsibility.

Maintaining ethical boundaries necessitates international collaboration. Regulating and monitoring technological advancements at the global level ensures that universal ethical standards are upheld. In areas such as artificial intelligence, autonomous systems, and genetic engineering, international regulations are crucial for building a safe and equitable future for humanity.

Social awareness must also be supported through education. Ethical issues and solutions related to technology should be integrated into educational curricula. Teaching younger generations to use technology responsibly and ethically can help create more conscientious individuals and communities in the future.

The environmental dimension is another essential component of ethical boundaries. The production and use of technology must account for its environmental impact. Sustainable manufacturing processes and the use of renewable energy sources can help ensure that technological progress does not come at the expense of the planet. Social awareness can encourage individuals to support these efforts by adopting eco-friendly technologies.

Ethical boundaries also play a significant role in interactions between humans and AI or robots. Human dignity and rights must be prioritized in these relationships. Preventing robots and AI systems from manipulating human emotions or controlling human behavior is critical to addressing potential ethical risks.

Social awareness is also necessary to address power imbalances in technology use. The gap between those who have access to technology and those who do not can exacerbate social inequalities. Therefore, technology must be distributed equitably, ensuring that its benefits are accessible to everyone.

Media and communication channels play a crucial role in fostering social awareness. Content that emphasizes ethical boundaries and the responsible use of technology can help individuals and communities become more sensitive to these issues. Additionally, media outlets must avoid spreading misinformation and adhere to ethical standards to support social awareness effectively.

In conclusion, ethical boundaries and social awareness are foundational to using technology for the benefit of humanity. Maximizing technology's potential requires individuals, corporations, and governments to work together with a shared understanding. By fostering awareness at every level of society, technology can evolve and be utilized responsibly within ethical boundaries, ensuring a positive impact on the world.

8.2.2. Responsibilities Toward the Future

Responsibilities toward the future have become increasingly critical in light of rapid technological advancements and the growing complexity of global challenges. Humanity must not only focus on addressing today's needs but also adopt a proactive approach to ensure the well-being, rights, and quality of life for future generations. These responsibilities span a wide range of stakeholders, including individuals, governments, international organizations, and the private sector.

The first and most fundamental responsibility is ensuring environmental sustainability. The depletion of natural resources, climate change, and environmental pollution pose significant threats to future human life. Actions taken today—such as promoting the use of renewable energy, encouraging recycling technologies, and adopting environmentally friendly production processes—are essential for leaving a more livable planet for future generations.

Education is another cornerstone of responsibilities toward the future. Equipping younger generations with technological skills is critical for adapting to evolving job markets. However, education should not be limited to technical knowledge; it must also integrate ethical values, critical thinking, and social awareness. This approach is vital for cultivating informed and responsible individuals.

The ethical use of technology is a key responsibility for the future. Fields such as artificial intelligence, big data, and biotechnology offer significant opportunities but also present ethical risks. These technologies must be directed in ways that respect human rights, promote social equity, and protect individual privacy.

Transparency, fairness, and accountability are essential principles in this context.

Ensuring social equality and increasing opportunities for all is another critical responsibility toward the future. The benefits of technological advancements are often accessible to specific groups, leaving others excluded. Policies that provide equal opportunities to all segments of society are essential to ensuring that technological progress benefits everyone.

Preserving cultural heritage is also an important responsibility for the future. Cultural values, traditions, and knowledge can be safeguarded and passed on to future generations through digital tools. However, this process must ensure that these values retain their meaning and context. Digitalization can help broaden the reach of cultural heritage, contributing to the preservation of humanity's history.

International cooperation plays a crucial role in fulfilling responsibilities toward the future. Global challenges have a transnational nature, requiring international regulations and collaborations for effective solutions. Issues such as climate change, pandemics, and cybersecurity cannot be addressed without collective efforts.

In conclusion, responsibilities toward the future are not limited to solving today's problems but also involve building a sustainable, equitable, and ethical world. Humanity can begin addressing these responsibilities today by fostering a collaborative effort to provide a better future for the generations to come. Cooperation among individuals, institutions, and governments is essential for achieving long-term success and ensuring that the future is brighter for all.

8.3. A NEW BEGINNING: THE SHARED FUTURE OF HUMANS AND ROBOTS

With the rapid advancement of technology, a shared future between humans and robots has become an inevitable reality. Artificial intelligence (AI) and robotics are no longer just tools to simplify lives; they are redefining human nature, social structures, and expectations for the future. This shared future represents a new beginning for humanity while also introducing significant responsibilities.

A world where humans and robots coexist requires a redefinition of interactions and relationships. As robots develop emotional and social intelligence, humans increasingly see them not only as tools but also as social partners. This evolution introduces new ethical dimensions to human-robot interactions.

This shared future is driving significant transformations, particularly in the workplace. Automation and AI optimize production processes while offering humans the opportunity to take on more creative and strategic roles. However, investments in education and skill development are essential to ensure that people are not left behind in this transformation.

Education plays a critical role in the shared future of humans and robots. Technology-enabled personalized learning tools can make learning processes more efficient for both humans and robots. For harmonious coexistence, humans must understand technology and acquire the skills necessary to work alongside robots.

Healthcare is another area where the shared future of humans and robots is making a significant impact. Robotic surgery, AI-powered diagnostic systems, and care robots are revolutionizing healthcare services. These collaborative models between humans and robots have the potential to transform patient care and medical innovation.

The shared future of humans and robots also brings profound changes to social life. Robots capable of providing emotional support and forming social bonds with humans have the potential to address modern issues such as loneliness. However, care must be taken to ensure that such interactions do not replace human-to-human relationships.

This shared future must be supported by ethical and legal regulations. Protecting human rights, ensuring fairness in the use of robots, and safeguarding privacy are critical for the sustainability of this new world. Additionally, the rights and responsibilities of robots must be clearly defined.

Environmental sustainability is another crucial issue in the shared future of humans and robots. The production and energy consumption of robots can have environmental impacts. Therefore, developing energy-efficient technologies and utilizing renewable resources are of paramount importance.

Preserving cultural values is also critical in a world shared by humans and robots. Robots' ability to adapt to and support different cultures can enhance social harmony. Additionally, robots have the potential to play a role in preserving and disseminating cultural heritage through digitalization.

Another dimension of this shared future is the redefinition of individual identity and human nature. The bonds formed with robots and their impact on the perception of identity could lead to deep philosophical debates in the future. Humanity may need to continuously redefine itself in its relationship with technology.

As robots gain independence in decision-making processes, new responsibilities emerge for humanity. Ensuring that robots make ethical and fair decisions highlights the importance of human oversight. Humans must act as guides in shaping the value systems of robots.

The shared future of humans and robots offers significant opportunities for economic growth and social welfare. Integrating robots into the workforce can increase production efficiency and accelerate economic growth. However, ensuring the equitable distribution of these benefits is critical to maintaining social balance.

Social equality is a fundamental aspect of building this shared future. Ensuring that the advantages of technology reach all segments of society is essential for long-term harmony and sustainability. This can only be achieved through the collective efforts of governments, companies, and individuals.

The shared future of humans and robots also requires global cooperation. Since this partnership transcends borders, international regulations and standards must be developed. Collaboration on issues such as ethics, security, and sustainability is essential at a global level.

In conclusion, the shared future of humans and robots is filled with immense opportunities and complex responsibilities. This new beginning requires ethical, fair, and sustainable approaches to ensure that technology becomes a supportive mechanism for humanity rather than a threat. Humanity must preserve its values while aligning technology with these principles.

In this future, the harmony between humans and robots will set new standards across all areas of life, creating a transformative process that expands the potential of humanity.

8.3.1. A Perspective on a World Where Humans and Robots Coexist

The rapid advancement of technology has made it possible for humans and robots to coexist in a shared future. This coexistence not only brings new opportunities and solutions but also introduces complex ethical, social, and philosophical questions. Humanity must adopt innovative approaches at both individual and societal levels to understand and guide this transformation.

The integration of robots into daily life is redefining human-robot relationships. Robots are no longer confined to factories or laboratories; they now exist in homes, offices, and even social spaces. People increasingly see robots not just as tools but as colleagues, assistants, or even social partners, creating a profound shift in human-robot interactions.

This shared world demands a reinterpretation of human nature. With technologies that enhance physical and mental capacities, humanity has the opportunity to transcend its limitations. However, this also sparks philosophical debates about what it means to be human, as human identity expands beyond biological traits.

Ethics is one of the most critical aspects of this coexistence. As robots develop autonomous decision-making abilities, clear ethical boundaries must be established. Humans must ensure that these machines are programmed and guided responsibly to protect individual rights and promote social harmony.

In education, the role of robots is rapidly expanding. AI-powered learning tools optimize individual learning processes and provide effective guidance to students. Robots as teachers or instructors open new doors in education, but it is essential to preserve human connections and the role of educators in this process.

In healthcare, the use of robots is revolutionizing treatment processes. Robotic surgery enables precise operations, AI-assisted diagnostic systems make healthcare more accessible, and care robots improve the quality of life for the elderly and disabled. This collaboration between humans and robots has transformative potential for medical innovation and patient care.

In the workplace, robots are reshaping productivity and redefining the role of human labor. Automation processes are transforming or eliminating many job sectors. Adapting to this new order requires continuous education and skill development to ensure that people remain relevant in the workforce.

Social relationships are undergoing significant transformation in a world where humans and robots coexist. As robots are increasingly accepted as social partners, there is a risk of replacing human-to-human interactions. It is vital to prioritize social bonds and recognize the irreplaceable need for human connections.

Robots are also making contributions to cultural life. Robots capable of creating art, literature, and music are changing the nature of cultural production. However, ethical frameworks must ensure that these creations are meaningful and align with human emotions and values.

Environmental impacts are another important consideration in the production and use of robots. Issues such as energy consumption and waste management must be addressed for environmental sustainability. Renewable energy sources and eco-friendly production methods can mitigate the negative effects in this area.

Legal regulations play a critical role in a world where humans and robots coexist. The legal status, responsibilities, and rights of robots must be clearly defined. These regulations are essential for preventing the misuse of technology and ensuring justice within society.

A world shared by humans and robots also calls for international cooperation. This coexistence can enhance the role of robots in solving global issues. Robots can make a significant difference in disaster management, health crises, and environmental emergencies, saving human lives and resources.

In conclusion, a world where humans and robots coexist offers immense opportunities and challenges. Humanity must approach this process ethically, fairly, and sustainably to ensure that technology becomes a tool for enhancing human potential and improving quality of life without replacing human values.

This new global order represents a transformation where humanity redefines its nature and its relationship with technology. A future where humans and robots work in harmony can open the door to a more equitable, sustainable, and creative way of life for all.